A KNIGHT AND HIS WEAPONS

By the same author:
A KNIGHT AND HIS ARMOUR
A KNIGHT AND HIS HORSE
A KNIGHT AND HIS CASTLE
A KNIGHT IN BATTLE
DARK AGE WARRIOR
THE ARCHAEOLOGY OF WEAPONS
THE SWORD IN THE AGE OF CHIVALRY

About the Author

Ewart Oakeshott was born in 1916. He began collecting swords while still in school at Dulwich, and has since built up a superb collection, specializing in the medieval period. His books include *The Archaeology of Weapons, European Weapons and Armour,* and *The Sword in the Age of Chivalry.* His books for children include the acclaimed 'Knight' series. He always brings to his books a wide and deep knowledge of his subject, and a witty and pithy style. The *Times Educational Supplement* rightly called him "one of those rarely gifted researchers who combine exhaustive investigation with absorbing enthusiasm." Oakeshott (and three friends) founded the Arms and Armour Society, a flourishing concern with a worldwide membership. His home is in Ely, close to Cambridge, England.

A KNIGHT
AND HIS WEAPONS

Second Edition

EWART OAKESHOTT F.S.A.
Illustrated by the author

Dufour Editions

First published 1964,
this revised second edition published 1997

Published in the United States of America by
Dufour Editions Inc.,
Chester Springs, Pennsylvania 19425

Library of Congress Cataloging-in-Publication Data

Oakeshott, R. Ewart.
    A knight and his weapons / Ewart Oakeshott ; illustrated
by the author. – 2nd ed.
        p.   cm.
    Includes bibliographical references and index.
    ISBN 0-8023-1299-3
    1. Weapons–Europe–History. 2. Armor, Medieval–History.
3. Military art and science–History–Medieval, 500-1500.
4. Military history, Medieval. 5. Knights and knighthood.
I. Title.
U810.01724   1997
623.4'41–dc21   97-36071
                                        CIP

ISBN 0-8023-1299-3

Printed and bound in the
United States of America

Contents

I. A KNIGHT AND HIS WEAPONS 7

II. SPEAR AND LANCE 19

III. AXE, MACE, AND HAMMER 41

IV. SWORD AND DAGGER 57

V. EARLY FIREARMS 95

  GLOSSARY 109

  BIBLIOGRAPHY 117

  INDEX 121

A Knight and His Weapons

The French knights had died by the hundreds along the hedge, beaten into the earth by the terrible hail of English arrows or struck down by sword and axe and mace wielded by English men-at-arms. They lay in twisted tangled heaps, men and horses together, either dead or wounded and feebly struggling to escape from the ghastly press of bodies. A few English archers and squires moved wearily about, searching for fallen comrades or helping wounded ones back into the shelter of the Nouaillé woods, but most simply sat or lay on the trampled ground. They were as still as their foes, exhausted by three long hours of battle. It was past noon now, and since nine o'clock that morning in 1356 the English force had beaten back two tremendous attacks by the great army of France.

Edward Plantagenet, Prince of Wales, sat on the ground with his back propped against a thorn tree. His beautiful black armor was dented now, dusty and battered, smeared with dark stains; his surcoat, blazoned with the arms of England and France, was cut to ribbons, its glowing color dimmed to a blotched red. His long sword lay across his knees, its bright blade horribly marred, its keen edge hacked and notched. His head drooped forward on his chest. He was weary and sick, so tired that he felt he would never move again. And he knew that over there, out of sight beyond the low ridge on the other side of the shallow vale of the battlefield, another great host of Frenchmen might yet be waiting to roll down upon his little, exhausted army. They had fought like demons, but now there were no more English arrows to stop or unnerve the French; weapons were broken and lost, armor so bent that it had to be discarded, visors torn from helmets – but worse than all that, his valiant English were so tired. Few had no wound upon them. They lacked food and in the dry, dusty fields their thirst was abominable.

The prince raised his head and, in spite of his fierce spirit, gazed longingly back to where the horses stood in the wagon-park behind his battle line. Perhaps they might get off, even now, if they were to mount and run for it. Holy Saints – he, Edward of Wales, to run for it! But what else could he do? His men were the cream of England's knighthood. He must save them from French prisons if he could.

Sick at heart he stared at the battleground. Had they finished with the French? There lay the broken remains of the mounted charge of the marshals, and of the dauphin's great "battle" which had rolled up to their hedge, only to be held and to break away in flight after hours of desperate fighting. But where was the division of the duc d'Orléans, and where was the French king? Edward groaned and eased his back. He lifted his eyes from the depressing sight below him, and gazed for relief at the dark woods beyond, their heavy summer green beautifully dappled with the reds and golds of autumn. He looked toward the blue sky, drawing deep breaths of the hot, still air, then shifted his gaze to the ridge to the north of the battlefield. He stiffened: a dazzling point of light flashed briefly from the ridge, twinkled, and flashed again. Then near it was another, and another. As he looked, the whole length of the ridge lit up with points of brilliance that grew and multiplied until he could see dots and flashes of bright color above them. There was an army there, then! A cracked voice broke the silence. "Oh, Holy St. Paul, look at that. It must be the king's division!" Edward looked at the speaker, one of his household knights, and caught his eye. The knight continued: "This is the end, sir. We're done for now!"

Edward's answer came like a crackle of lightning. "You lie! No one shall say we're beaten while I stand!" His spurt of anger lifted him to his feet, but once upright he nearly fell. John Chandos, his friend and chief-of-staff, propped himself on an elbow. Looking up at the prince he cocked one eyebrow and croaked, "Faith, sir, you'll not stand either unless you sit. We must mount if we're to fight any more today."

For a moment Edward looked over at the French position, where the unwearied thousands of King Jean's division had halted on the ridge-top. Then: "By God, John, you've hit it. We'll mount, archers and all – there'll be horses for everyone now – and we'll charge 'em – take them when they get to that broken tree – see, down there in the bottom. They won't expect it. Look at those men of theirs, pulling out the wounded. They've been sending people back and forth ever since the last attack. They must know what poor shape we seem to be in. Come on, John – up with you, and go along the line and tell 'em – get hold of Warwick and Salisbury. Talk to the company commanders, make 'em see what I want. They'll catch the idea soon enough, tired as they are." He stirred a recumbent body with his foot: "Hey, Thomas! Wake up. Go back to the wagon-park and tell them to bring the horses forward. Quick, now. There's no time to lose. Get moving, lads, or you'll be too stiff to mount!"

Calling in his cheery voice, Edward strode out from the shade of his little tree along the line of beaten-looking men. "Come on, boys – the king of

France'll be along this way in a minute. Who's going to capture him for me?" The afternoon sun glowed on his sweat-darkened chestnut hair, and where he passed his men stirred with new life. All along the line of the flattened hedge they were coming to their feet, stretching, fastening loosened armor, picking up helmets and weapons. Cracked voices, weary but cheerful, rose into the still air, competing with the horrid sounds that still came from those mournful, tangled heaps.

By the time he had reached the center of the line, the horses had been brought up, along with what little store of water there was; each man had just enough to ease his terrible thirst. Everywhere men were mounting, some without helmets, others lacking vambraces. Many had taken off their leg harness to fight more easily on foot. The squires and pages brought fresh lances, but there were so few spares that many knights went over the dead men in search of weapons, and the archers pulled arrows out of the bodies. The prince's horse was brought to him where he stood talking to the earls of Warwick and Salisbury, who commanded the two main divisions of the army. As he put his foot in the stirrup to mount, he looked over his shoulder toward the French. Their whole line shimmered again with points of light, winking and flashing in the bright sun.

"Now, by St. Paul!" the prince yelled, "they're

coming. Up, lads, and be ready for 'em!" He leaped into his saddle and cantered back to his own command post, a little to the left of the line. By the thorn tree his household knights awaited him. One handed up his helmet; another gave him his gauntlets. John Chandos, who had not yet mounted, gave him his battered sword. "Not much good now, sir," he grinned, "but I don't doubt you'll be able to make some use of it!" "Ha, John, I'd have liked a fresh one, but it'll have to do, won't it? If it's too bad I can use my little axe, here. Come on now, up with you. They're nearly where we want them. Now – " He turned to one of his Gascon captains, Sir Jean de Grailly, in command of the small reserve – "Sir Jean, I want you to take as many knights as you can – you've about sixty of your own following, haven't you? – and my reserve, archers and all, and go round behind that little hill over there to the right. When we meet the French down there in that field – you see that broken tree? – come you in like all the devils in hell on their flank. Make plenty of noise, and come hard. So God speed you. Trumpeter – be ready to blow when I tell you."

He looked keenly along the line, at the tired men transformed by the thought of aggressive action at last after standing all the morning on the defensive; now that they had their horses, all their tiredness seemed to have gone. In the tense silence someone could be heard singing, and where the archers of the earl of Warwick's "battle" rode there was a sudden burst of laughter. Then all was quiet again save for the song and a dull, jingling thunder of sound, growing steadily on the warm air – the feet of thousands of armored Frenchmen trudging across the fields.

Suddenly Edward stood up in his stirrups. His voice, high and ringing, could be heard all along the battle-line: "St. George! St. George! Forward, banner!" followed instantly by the harsh blare of trumpets and the rattle of drums sounding the charge. Slowly at first, picking their way at a walk to avoid the slain, Edward's little army moved forward. Out in the open fields beyond the heaps of wreckage the pace quickened, first to an amble, then to a canter. A hundred yards from the enemy the fluttering pennons on the lances slowly sank down as the twinkling, deadly points were leveled; then the canter became a run, the swift smooth gait of charging coursers. Men were shouting now – war cries, curses, or just noises – until, with a tremendous howling crash that the citizens of Poitiers seven miles away heard clearly, the two lines met. Many of the English went down, but the mounted men plunged on, deep into the weltering mass of their foes, following the banner of England where it surged and tossed above the fight, out in front of the line. Soon the charge was halted, and the battle became a ferocious mêlée. In the center of his division fought the French king, Jean the Good Fellow, with his little son Philippe fighting like a tiger cub at his side. For a long while the French held on, their close-packed ranks engulfing the English. But gradually from the rear in ones and twos men began to go back; the whole mass was wavering under the pressure of the mounted English. Then there was a shock to the left of the French: yells and screams, the savage neighing of horses and the persistent blare of a trumpet. The French gave ground more quickly now, and soon whole groups of them were stumbling frantically back to get to their horses. Only round the king a solid body of French knights fought stubbornly on, hemmed in now on all sides by their triumphant adversaries.

The prince and his household had cut their way into the French army until there was no one before them. Then Edward would have turned back into the fight, but Chandos and the others persuaded him to stop. His banner was hoisted high into a cherry tree in a cottage garden in Maupertuis village to serve as a rallying point for his men, who were now reaping a rich harvest of prisoners from the defeated French, and pursuing those who fled toward Poitiers.

Suddenly a noisy group broke through the milling crowd, making toward the prince. In their midst, jostled and thrust roughly along, was a knight in rich, battered armor and a small boy.

From where he sat on his horse Edward could see over the heads of the quarreling men who hustled them so rudely along. "It's the king! John, Robert — look, they've got the king!" Edward kicked his tired horse forward. His voice, cracking with weariness, rang out like a whiplash. "Stop! Stop, I tell you! Is this how you treat a king? God's dignity, I'll hang the next man that touches him! Make way for me." He lit down from his horse, staggering with exhaustion, and by the sheer blaze of his anger clove a way through the press until he came face to face with the king of France. Down Edward went on his knee. "Sire," he said, "my apologies that you have been treated so. Come with me now and rest. My tent will be pitched in a few minutes. Please do me the honor of sharing it with me." He stood up and put out his hand to touch the boy's shoulder. "This is my cousin, Philippe, isn't it?" Edward's smile was warm and full of charm, but the boy drew angrily away. His small, dirty face was as white as a bone, his dark eyes glaring savagely in the shadows of his raised visor. The king spread his hands helplessly. "Philippe, this is not courteous. Your cousin is a great captain." The king sighed. "Too great for poor France ... treat him properly." Edward put his arm around the king's shoulders. "There, don't chide him, sir. It's a hard thing to be taken in battle, and a poor way for cousins to meet. I don't doubt I look horrible, too. Come away now and rest."

That was at Poitiers, on September 19, 1356, the hardest and best-fought of England's great victories in the Hundred Years' War against France. Crécy in 1346 and Agincourt in 1415 were won mostly by the archers and their terrible weapon, but at Poitiers the English won against huge odds by sheer guts, hard slogging, and the fiery genius of the great commander, Edward, Black Prince of Wales. One of the finest moments in England's history was when that tired, near-beaten little army mounted for that last unforgettable charge which gave them victory and made France's king their prisoner. The political results of that battle were far more important than any of the others: that the whole war was a seemingly pointless aggression need not dim the glory of that afternoon. It was in the years following that Edward showed himself to be a military leader equal to great dukes and earls, some of whom outshone famous kings as the sun outshines the moon.

Despite the 641 years that have passed since the day of Poitiers, and the 621 since Edward's death in 1376, we still have links to him. For instance, the hand with which I write these words has worn the gauntlet of the Black Prince, one which he might have been wearing during that splendid charge, and the eyes with which I see the page have looked, as his did, through the eye-slits of his great jousting helmet. To be able to handle these precious things in this way is a privilege rarely granted, but they can be seen in Canterbury Cathedral, where for centuries they hung above his tomb. Luckily for us, in 1954 exact replicas of all these things were made, so that the now fragile originals could be kept in safety in a glass case, while the replicas hang above the tomb.

Resting atop this tomb is a splendid effigy in gilt bronze of the prince in full armor. Among the personal gear surviving is part of his sword's scabbard; the sword itself used to be there, but it has been missing since the English Civil War of the seventeenth century. The scabbard is little more than a tattered relic, but at the side of the effigy is a most beautiful sword in bronze gilt; the sheath is decorated with red and blue enamel, and in the pommel is a little lion's mask picked out in blue enamel. Figure 1 (pg. 18) shows what the weapon was like.

The battle of Poitiers was fought with the various weapons of the men-at-arms. Though there were several thousand English bowmen and French crossbowmen present, their missiles had comparatively little effect on the battle. The English arrows were all used up in the first two attacks, while the French commanders placed their crossbowmen so badly that they were rarely able to engage at all. It was sheer hard slogging with lance and sword, axe and mace, and war-hammer.

Fig. 1. Effigy of the Black Prince in Canterbury Cathedral showing sword in detail

Spear and Lance

The spear is one of the earliest weapons. Some 20,000 years ago a sharp flint lashed to a stick served to bring down game for the cooking-pot, or

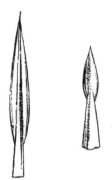

an enemy for personal satisfaction. This crude tool developed into the beautifully wrought flints of the New Stone Age, some 6,000 years ago, and then to the lovely bronze spears made as recently as some 3,500 years ago (fig. 2).

The knight's spear was of course the long lance, but before we consider it we ought to look at some spears that preceded it to see how they were used. There is little variation in the shape of a spearhead. Forms in use when Pharaoh's power dominated the lands of the

Fig. 2. Bronze spearhead, c. 1000 B.C., and right, Iron spearhead, Celtic, c. 300 B.C.

Eastern Mediterranean are similar to the ones popular when Queen Victoria's power dominated India, and in the 3,000 years in between we find many forms constantly repeated from Wales to Japan and from Finland to Morocco.

In ancient Greece (from about 600 B.C. to 120 B.C.), one way of using the spear on foot was to hurl it from a distance of only a few feet. A warrior tried to hit his enemy in the midriff. As the warrior threw, he ran in; his foe doubled up over the spear in his stomach as the warrior finished him with a strong sword-stroke to the back of the neck as the foe went forward. If the warrior missed with his first throw, he might be lucky enough to cast his second spear and get his enemy with that.

The Romans developed a very specialized form of throwing-spear for this purpose, called a pilum. Its head was small and leaf-shaped, set on a very long iron neck which ended in a hollow socket into which the shaft of ash or acacia wood was set (fig. 3). The reason for the slender iron neck below the head was this: when the legionary engaged with a foe, he flung his pilum as he advanced. If it hit the foe's shield the spear stuck into it, but the iron shaft bent down-

Fig. 3.
Pilum

20

ward. The unlucky foe would then have to cope with a heavy bent spear dragging his shield down. Of course, the simplest and best solution would have been to hack off the stuck spear near the head with an axe or sword, but the iron neck made this impossible.

This spear type was adopted by the Franks and Anglo-Saxons, who called it an angon, and they used it in precisely the same way, to deprive their enemy of the use of his shield – if, of course, they did not get through or behind the shield to wound or kill him.

Greek and Roman cavalrymen – who rode without the support of stirrups – used the same sort of spear as foot soldiers, a fairly light one with a long, sharp-pointed head, but never the pilum. They did not tuck it under their arm to charge with, like a lance, but held it free at arm's length, for it was too short to use effectively held in close; and sometimes they hurled it.

The Vikings and their predecessors used many varieties of spear, each with its own name, such as a hewing-spear, a string-spear (one which was thrown by a loop of cord wound round the shaft), a javelin, and so on. Well-preserved examples of these different spears have been found in Denmark, many of the string-spears still having their loops of cord attached. The Vikings used fanciful and poetic descriptive phrases for their weapons; spears were often called "Serpent," "Serpent of Blood," "Serpent of the Warlinden" (the shield), and so on. Mail shirts were likened to nets – a very apt description for the hard mesh of mail: for instance, they were called "Net of the Spears," while the spear would be called "Fish of the War-net." Sometimes it was attractively named "The Flying Dragon of the Fight."

Fig. 4. Winged spears, 9th century A.D., and right, winged spear, late 15th century

The spear was used by foot-soldiers during all the long centuries between the time of the Sumerians of about 3000 B.C. and the end of the Thirty Years' War in Europe in A.D. 1648. Sumerian and Egyptian foot-soldiers used a broad-bladed weapon about six feet long; they fought with it like a bayoneted rifle, in disciplined bodies of infantry acting in close formation and charging in line. The same sort of weapon was used by the Franks, Saxons, and Vikings, and by the Scots at Bannockburn in 1314 and by the French at Poitiers in 1356, as well as by the professional Welsh and

Brabançon spearmen in the armies of the four-teenth and fifteenth centuries. The head of this spear – whether it was used by the infantry of Pharaoh, Themistocles, Sweyn Forkbeard, Robert Bruce, or Charles the Rash – was of the same shape: about ten to twelve inches long, broad at the base – some two or even three inches – with a strong rib running up the middle. In the Middle Ages, particularly during the eighth and ninth centuries, and again in the fifteenth, the spear was often furnished with wings or lugs below the head, made as part of the socket (fig. 4). This broad spear could be used as both a cutting and a thrusting weapon.

Another specialized form of infantry spear was the pike, purely a thrusting weapon with a different shaped head set on an extremely long shaft, often as much as eighteen feet long. This head was small and nar-

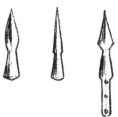

Fig. 5. Pike-heads, c. 1500

row, only about six inches long and hardly broad-er than the shaft behind it (fig. 5). The pike was first used in ancient Greece in the armies of Macedon about 300-120 B.C. and was developed – or rather, its tactical use was developed – by the ruler of that land, Philip, father of Alexander the Great. It dom-inated the art of war in those areas of the Middle

East conquered by Alexander until in 168 B.C. it met the Roman legions at Pydna. Here the pilum and short sword in the hands of the tough legionaries completely overcame the pike, and we hear no more of it until the Swiss reintroduced it during the 15th century A.D. Then, like the ancient Macedonians, they dominated the battlefields of Europe with it until, in a great and bloody battle at Bicocca in Northern Italy in 1522, they were decisively beaten by the firepower of the newly perfected arquebus.

The reason for the great length of the pike was so that three or even four ranks of the column could have their pike-heads projecting in front: the front-rank men held their pikes low, the butt resting on the ground behind them; the second rank presented its pikes between the front-rank men, holding their pikes level, while those in the third rank held them high and presented them over the shoulders of the front-rank men (fig. 6). The ranks behind held their pikes upright, ready to step for-

Fig. 6. Pikemen in Formation

ward and take the place of men who fell in the leading ranks. Thus arrayed, the whole column, often about 2,000 men, rolled irresistibly forward. Until it became possible to thin out these columns with cannon and arquebus fire before they came to close quarters, nothing could stand before them except another column of pikes. Then came the "push of pikes," when the two columns, locked together, pushed at each other like linemen in a football game until one or the other gave way.

There were many other spearlike weapons, all of the same family and true descendants of the paleolithic hunter's flint. They were not used by knights of the Middle Ages, but were used against them by foot-soldiers and were the direct cause of changes in knightly armor. So they should be mentioned here. All of them spring from a marriage between the military spear and the agricultural bill-hook. This tool, very simple and effective for chopping

Fig. 7.
Modern
bill-hook

objects, trimming hedges and so on, is still made today in the same shapes as it had 800 years ago (fig. 7). It is a traditional object, and in England its form varies according to the place it is made in – a Westmorland bill-hook is distinct from a Gloucestershire one, and so on, though all are of the same basic design. When a bill-hook is mount-

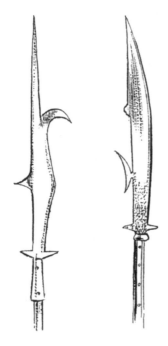

Fig. 8. Glaive-heads. Glaive or Bill, c. 1470, and right, another form of glaive, c 1550

ed on a long shaft, it becomes a weapon, and it was often used in this way by infantry throughout the earlier part of the Middle Ages. Until about 1300 it was just a bill-hook on a pole, but around this time the marriage with the spear took place. The resulting offspring were, so to speak, two brothers, called glaive and halberd. The glaive developed a long spear-like spike in front and another shorter one on the back of the blade, which itself became longer and narrower (fig. 8). The halberd had a much broader, shorter blade, with a similar spike in front – in fact, it became like a great axe on a five-foot haft. (Incidentally, when talking of the poles upon which spears, axes, glaives, halberds, and so on were mounted, we use the word "shaft" for spears and lances, and "haft" for axes and halberds and the like.)

These weapons developed during the four-

teenth and fifteenth centuries. The glaive (called a
bill in England) became very elegant and sophisticated, while the halberd, having by about 1470
reached a peak of efficient design (fig. 9A), began
rapidly to decline after about 1525 into a merely
decorative and cere-
monial object. The
halberds of the time
of Elizabeth I were
very handsome, but
hardly of any use for
fighting (fig. 9B). In
fact, they were only
used to make a good
show in the hands of
state or city guards.

Between about
1400 and 1600 the
spear also devel-
oped several differ-
ent forms. These were given many names in
medieval times, and it is now very difficult to sort
out which name applied to which weapon: vouge,
ranseur, gisarme, runka, and so on. The vouge was
probably the same thing as the glaive; the ranseur
could be any kind of bill-like weapon, while the
gisarme has been taken to be a very large and
beautiful spear which reached its full development
at the same time as the halberd, about 1470. It is

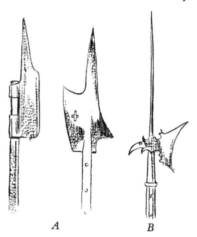

A   *B*

Fig. 9. Halberds
A, c. 1470 and B, c. 1570

27

more often called a partisan, with a big head, like a great, broad sword-blade. Generally about 30 inches long, it is very broad at the base (called the shoulders of the blade), where it spreads out into a small wing or lug on each side (fig. 10). These are different from the lugs on the winged spear mentioned earlier, for in that weapon the lugs are separate from the blade and placed below it on the socket, whereas in the partisan they spring from the blade itself. Tens of thousands of these partisans were made plain for fighting, but many were elaborately and beautifully decorated with etching and gilding, or damascening in gold and silver, for ceremo-

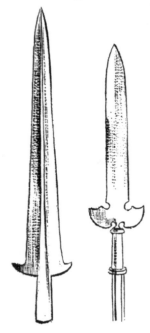

Fig. 10. Partisan, c. 1470, and right, c. 1600

nial use by the personal guards of magnates. As time went on, the blade became smaller and the lugs larger, until the device developed the form in which it is still used today: for instance, by the yeoman warders of the Tower of London on ceremonial occasions. These ceremonial partisans – indeed, nearly all ceremonial hafted weapons –

have a large tassel fitted on the top of the haft just below the blade. Such a fitting was often applied, too, to the fighting varieties of the weapon and had a practical purpose – it soaked up any blood that might run off the blade, preventing such blood from running down the haft and making it sticky.

These infantry weapons, though used for a long time, had little effect on the course of medieval battles, which were usually decided by the heavy cavalry – the men-at-arms and the knights. But early in the fourteenth century the halberd, newly developed by the Flemings and the Swiss, had a great deal of influence on the development of the armor these men-at-arms and knights wore. In two battles, at Courtrai in Flanders (1302) and Morgarten in Switzerland (1315), large forces of splendidly equipped cavalry were terribly defeated by townsmen and peasants armed with halberds.

At Courtrai the best of France's knighthood, armed with lance and sword and protected by mail reinforced at the knee and shoulder with iron plate, and with coats of plates under their surcoats, made a series of gallant but badly organized charges across a stream against a solid mass of Flemings. Two things happened that the French knights did not expect. First, the townsmen stood firm and did not break and run before the proud trampling horses. Second, the mounted charges got bogged down in the muddy meadow between the stream and the Flemings' position; while they were floundering about trying to get up speed to charge the enemy ranks, the Flemings themselves took the initiative and charged the knights who were at such a disadvantage. The halberds (these Flemings called them godendags – "good mornings") cut through the knightly mail and clove shield and helmet as a knife goes through butter.

It was the French knights who broke and tried to run, but they had to struggle through the muddy field with the stream at its bottom. In panic and disorder they crowded down to the water. Those who reached it first tried to rein in and move aside to find a shallower place to cross, but they were pushed down the slippery bank by the crowds pushing behind; in they plunged, drowning by the hundreds in the muddy water.

At Morgarten a similar thing happened. The reasons for the battle are too complicated to go into in detail here. But, in brief, it began because in 1314 two rival emperors had been elected to the throne of the Holy Roman Empire, and one of the cantons of Switzerland, Schwyz, had decided to make use of the confusion to break away from the Empire and become independent. The brother of one of the emperors, Duke Leopold of Austria, was sent with a force of knights to bring the Schwyzers back to their allegiance. So one November day in

1314, this force was making its way through the mountains to come at this upland country. The Schwyzers had blocked all the roads save one, and along this the Austrians came, foolishly confident and unprepared. The road wound between a steep hillside and a small lake, and where the space between hill and lake was narrowest the Schwyzers blocked this road too, and set an ambush on the wood-crowned hill above. They cut a lot of tree-trunks, and trimmed the branches off close so that they would roll. Then they waited.

The head of the Austrian column came in sight. Suspecting nothing, for they had sent no scouts forward, the Austrians came happily on until they were stopped by the road-block. Those in front halted, but the rest of the column, not see-ing what was happening, came crowding up behind, quite filling the narrow meadow between the lake and the foot of the slope. There the mounted men milled about, the lake on their left and the slope crowned with sleeping autumn woods on their right. Suddenly from these quiet woods came a terrible yelling of war cries; down the slope plunged the rolling tree-trunks, crashing into the Austrian horses. And behind the logs charged the Swiss. In a few seconds they were upon the horrified Austrian knights, slashing and striking with their terrible halberds, shearing through helms as if they were made of paper.

Mailed arms and legs were hacked off; gallant horses were decapitated. The surprised knights fought like tigers, but there was little they could do. They could not turn and retreat, as the crowd was so close-packed. Those who were not cut down were forced into the lake; a few, by using their big war-swords to beat the halberds aside, were able to cut their way out to the rear and get away. For a few minutes the whole force stood, but as it became clear that the Swiss were complete masters of the situation, those Austrians in the rear of the column who had not been engaged turned their horses and made off, leaving more than half their force slaughtered on one of the most bloody of medieval battlefields.

After these two battles it became clear to military men that the old armor of mail, even if reinforced with a few pieces of plate, was not enough. Though it had proved completely effective against all previous weapons, it was no use against this new and terrible thing. More reinforcement was added. Plate now covered legs and arms, over the mail, and the wearing of a coat of plates over the mail shirt became essential; and mail itself was made stronger. A knight's equipment thus got heavier and more clumsy.

Then, in the 1340s, the armies of France met the English longbow and the dreadful yard-long arrows. Even this reinforced armor was not good against these weapons, as was most dreadfully proved at Crécy in 1346. Afterward it was plain that something better must be devised, so a complete, close-fitting armor of beautifully shaped plates of glass-hard iron was designed. By the late 1350s this sort of armor was worn by properly fitted men-at-arms all over Europe, and even the longbow arrows could not pierce it.

Whatever the armor they may have worn, knights' arms remained basically the same; the lance was still the knightly weapon par excellence, and was, of course, the weapon of that most knightly exercise, the joust, the running-together of two horsemen in single combat. I have described this elsewhere so will do no more here than to say something about the lances used for jousting and how they were used.

In earlier times – that is, from the days of the Goths in the fourth and fifth centuries until the time of the Black Prince in the fourteenth century, the shaft of the lance was simply a long, tapering pole between nine and eleven feet long, with a small head not unlike a pike-head which varied a good deal in shape (fig. 11). This variation does not

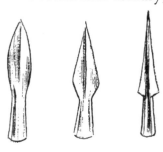

Fig. 11. Lance-heads, 14th-15th century

seem to have been a matter of period; all the varieties were in use together throughout the Middle Ages. It seems likely that the variation went by locality, as it does today in the case of bill-hooks, and that a Bordeaux lance might be of a shape totally different from a Cologne one, or a Milanese from both.

Not until very late in the Middle Ages did lances have any sort of guard for the hand. During the fourteenth century we find pictures and carvings that show a sort of short cross-guard like a sword-hilt in front of the hand, but not until the second quarter of the fifteenth century – that is,

Fig. 12. Vamplate, c. 1450

after about 1425 and later than Henry V – was the vamplate used. It is a large disk of iron fastened to the lance shaft that runs through its center, as a guard for the hand, which grips just behind it (fig. 12). You may see innumerable modern illustrations in historical stories of Normans and Crusaders going about with vamplates on their lances, but this is totally wrong.

At about the same time other attachments to the lance were introduced. The butt-end became much thicker, so a narrower piece had to be carved out for the hand-grip, and a rest was provided to take some of the lance's weight. This was a stout steel bracket bolted on to the right side of the breastplate, and you could rest your lance in it just in front of the vamplate, thus transferring some of the weight to the body. This rest was first used around 1400. Sixty years or so later, when special armor for jousting had been fully developed, a long queue, or tail, was fitted to the backplate. This projected about a foot or more out of the right side of the back, with a curled-over end under which the butt of the lance could be wedged. Thus, with the rest in front and the queue behind, most of the weight was transferred to the body-armor. When the queue was used, a graper was fastened round the lance behind the hand-grip. This was a solid disk of iron a little larger in diameter than the lance itself, its lower or rearmost rim toothed so it could catch firmly into the queue.

A special sort of lance-head was used in friendly jousts "à plaisance." It was called a cronel, a crown-shaped thing with three blunt prongs set wide apart to give the lance a grip on shield or helm, enough to overthrow a rider without piercing any part of his armor. Such heads came into use late in the twelfth century; they were called, back then, "lances of courtesy."

There are as many ways of using a spear when fighting on foot as there are types of spearhead, but there is really only one way to use the great lance. It is too long and heavy to hold free at arm's length; you must tuck it under your right arm and hold it steady against your chest. When you do this, it will incline over to the left across your body at an angle of thirty degrees because of the shape of your ribs; if you hold it really tight, as you must, it will not naturally project straight out in front of you on your right side. In another place I have dealt with the position used in jousting with the lance, but it is important to remember that in the Middle Ages it was always held thus, diagonally across the chest, projecting between a knight and his horse's neck, with the point on the knight's left front.

A knight had to be careful that this angle was not made too obtuse, for if it was too far to the left he could easily be swept out of his saddle by the shaft of his lance, never mind his opponent's point when the two knights struck. The shock of two armored knights running together was tremendous, and all that speed and weight was concentrated into the tiny point of the lance-head. Often the shaft of the lance broke with the stroke, but if it didn't, your armor had to be stout indeed to prevent the point splitting you. In the days of mail your stout shield of leather and wood took the main brunt of the blow, but later in the time of plate-armor, shields were not used. The glass-hard, smooth, rounded surfaces of the plate made even the most powerful blow glance off. All the overlapping of these plates was arranged so that each overlap was away from the direction of any blow; thus very few places remained where a lance-point could catch and tear your armor open.

A great deal of practice was necessary in jousting, more perhaps than in any other knightly use of arms; not only must you control your horse – also carefully trained – so that he runs straight and unswerving to pass his opponent close upon his near side, but you must aim your lance true at the point of the opponent which you must select as you run at him. Then, at the last split second before the impact, you have to brace yourself, rise in your stirrups, and thrust with your whole body as the shock comes. You also have to hold your shield very firm, and at an angle so that your assailant's lance will slide away off to your left side; and you must observe, in that last moment, where he aims to hit you. If he is going for your head, you have to move your great helm to take the blow glancing. All this calls for far more skill and far quicker reaction than almost anything else.

In the great battles of the Hundred Years' War during the fourteenth and fifteenth centuries, knights often fought on foot. When they did, their lances were almost useless, for they were too long to use in the rifle-bayonet fashion that a spear had to be used in. So they cut the shafts down to a manageable length. At Poitiers, all the French knights who fought on foot cut their lances down to about six feet. We read too of how they took off their foot-armor and cut the long points off their riding-boots – a thing you wear in armor even if you have a plated sabaton over it – so that they could walk more easily. They were not long boots, because of the greaves (armor for the shin and calf) which the knights wore, but short ones, such as worn with jodhpurs.

The methods of training to fight with the lance were simple. The basic need is to run at something and hit it true with your lance-point. The best known exercise is riding at the quintain. This is a contraption made by setting a vertical post in the ground; on top of this, set at right angles and swinging on a pivot, is a long cross-piece about seven feet above the ground. On one end is fastened a target – often fashioned and painted to represent a Saracen – and at the other is a sand-bag. If you hit the target in the right place, it swings the pole halfway round to let you pass; but if you don't hit it squarely, it swings right round and the sand-bag clouts you on the back as you go by.

A less amusing but probably far more practical method of practice was to run at a ring; you hang a small ring of rope, or anything a ring can be made of, from a tree-branch, and try to pick it up on your lance-point. You can do the same with a bit of cloth – or, if you want to do it today, an empty tin will do, or any small target that is hard to hit and will stay on your lance-point when you do hit it.

Another kind of knightly spear was for boar-hunting, one of the most risky and highly regarded exercises in the hunting field. Until late in the fifteenth century an ordinary spear like the infantry winged spear was used, but after about 1460 a special boar spear was devised. It had a large, broad, leaf-shaped blade, at the bottom of which a short bar was inserted in a hole, set at right angles to the plane of the blade (fig. 13). This was absolutely essential in a boar spear, for when you kill a charging boar you have to stand your ground before him, holding your spear firmly at the level of his chest.

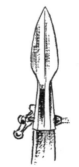

Fig. 13. Boar spear, c. 1500

He will run straight at you without swerving, nearly two hundred pounds of slavering, red-eyed ferocity, armed with seven-inch tusks which can disembowel you in a split second, coming at about twenty miles an hour. If your nerve is steady and your eye true, your point will take him low in the chest, but unless your spearhead has a bar across it he will not stop, but run right on up the spear even though it passes through him from end to end, bowl you over, and gore you as he dies. The bar stops him a spear's length away, though heaven knows, with a six-foot weapon and only three feet of it projecting in front of you, that is near enough.

Boar hunting in this way is undoubtedly a dangerous game. Some men used a sword, either like a spear – surely the most dangerous way of all – or in the way the notorious and rather glorious Cesare Borgia used to kill boars: he would stand waiting the charge of his boar, and then like a skilled toreador with a bull, he would swerve aside and cut the animal's head off with a single stroke as it tore past. This is not only more dangerous than with a spear, but infinitely more difficult. If you move too late you are done for; if you miss your stroke and only wound the boar, he can turn in a flash and come back at you from a different angle before you can get your balance. One does not wonder that men who were good at this were considered the most courageous of warriors.

Axe, Mace, and Hammer

The weapons I am going to discuss in this chapter we might call the secondary armament of medieval knights: axe, mace, and hammer. These weapons were often carried, as were the lance and sword, the main armament. Some individuals, of course, always preferred one or another of these usually secondary weapons to their swords, but the axe, mace, or hammer was most often used if the sword were broken or lost, or in very close fighting when the sword was too long to be effective.

The axe had always been a main armament weapon with infantry, particularly with those Northern races – Anglo-Saxons, Franks, and Vikings – who always fought on foot. The mace was simply a sophisticated club; often during the fifteenth century it was most beautifully made, very elegant and shapely. The same was true of the hammer, though we have no surviving examples of war-hammers that date from before 1380.

Many hammers from around 1380 until about 1560 do survive, however, and some are lovely weapons, both to look at and to handle.

Perhaps the best way to understand the significance of these three types of weapons is to look at each one separately and discuss its origins, development, and usage.

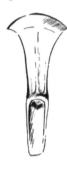

Fig. 14.
Bronze-age axe

The axe, like the spear, was one of the earliest weapons; a knight took his sharp flint, and fixed it with a lashing at right angles onto a short haft. The flint itself was about the same shape as the spearhead, which of course was made into a spear by fixing it as a point to a long shaft. During the New Stone Age finely wrought axe-heads were made, paving the way for the lovely and efficient bronze axes of the succeeding period (fig. 14). When iron became the usual material out of which weapons were made, axes became larger, and some of the best ones surviving from the period between 400 B.C. and A.D. 400 are from Scandinavia. It is no wonder the Vikings were such axe-men considering how popular the axe had always been with their ancestors. The Celtic peoples of Western Europe, however, seem not to have favored the axe; their weapon was the long sword.

An axe as a weapon is a difficult thing to define; it is a tool as well and can be easily used either way. In early times this seems to have been very much the case. Few of the thousands of ancient axes in our museums and collections can be unmistakably classified as war-axes. One type of axe, however, which could not be used for any purpose other than its military one was the little throwing-axe of the Franks, the "Francisca," from which the whole people got their name. This was a

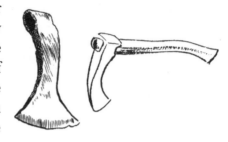

Fig. 15. Francisca, two examples, 7th century

small weapon, a little curved head on a very short haft (fig.15). The early Franks – before the time of Charlemagne – began a battle by making a furious charge at a run, yelling like maniacs and letting fly with their axes and angons as soon as they came within range of their targets. They then would use swords or, very often, big long-hafted axes to close on their enemy. I have one of these large axe-heads, found in the grave of an eighth-century warrior: it weighs about 2½ pounds and on its own is a very heavy-seeming lump of iron; but I wanted to see what it felt like as an axe; so I got a felling-axe haft and mounted my Frankish head on it. At once it came to life, and though it is too heavy for me to use in comfort with one hand, in both hands it is a marvelously balanced and effective weapon (fig. 16). These axe-hafts, by the way, are like bill-hooks: their shape has not altered with the passing of the centuries. That beautiful double curve is put into the wood not for its looks, but because that is how an axe-haft has to be.

Fig. 16. Frankish axe, 8th century

The Scandinavians of the pre-Viking age used axe-heads very similar in form to the Frankish ones; the only difference was in the socket. It is almost impossible to explain in words, so I will not try. Let the illustration (fig. 17) do it for me. You can see, small though this difference is, that it is very definite, and clearly distinguishes a Frankish axe from a Norse one.

It was not until the actual age of the Vikings, about 750-1000 A.D. that the great, broad-bladed axe was developed (fig. 18), and it seems to have been used only by the Vikings. One might think, to see pictures of these enormous axes with their beautifully curved edges between nine and thirteen inches long, that they must be very heavy, but they are not. They are so thin and finely wrought that they weigh no more than the more chunky earlier ones we have just looked at. They are far lighter

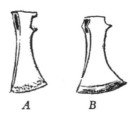

Fig. 17. Axe-sockets
A, Frankish;
B, Scandinavian

and easier to wave round your head than a modern felling-axe.

This form of axe-head remained in use right up into the thirteenth century. It was used mostly by foot-soldiers but often enough by mounted men-at-arms and knights. A good example of its use was at the battle of Lincoln in 1141. England's King Stephen – a very ineffectual king, but a most charming person and a fine and gallant knight – was captured while fighting with his army against the forces of his rival for England's crown, his cousin Queen Matilda. In the winter of 1140-41, Stephen captured the city of Lincoln from Matilda's supporters; but while he was inside the walls, a force collected by the earls of Gloucester and Chester marched to the city's relief.

Fig. 18. Viking axe,
11th century

45

Stephen decided to fight rather than be besieged. So he drew up his army outside the city, a little to the west of it. The army of the earls had to cross a flooded dike (this was in February) and fight with it at their backs in a position where defeat would have meant disaster. Both armies fought for the most part on foot, with only small forces of cavalry to begin the action. Stephen and the knights of his household dismounted to fight round the standard, as did the leaders of the earl's host.

The cavalry charge which began the battle ended in the complete rout of the king's men. Then the rest of the rebel army concentrated on the king's infantry. Chester assailed them in front while Gloucester and his "battle" beset them in the flanks and rear. The Royalists made a gallant resistance, but soon the mass was split up. The citizens of Lincoln made a bolt for their city gates, where their foes promptly followed them and cut them up in the streets. But Stephen and his followers stood firm by the standard and held out long after the rest of the fighting was over. The king fought like a lion, holding his enemies at bay around him. Then his sword broke. One of the Lincoln men who had stood by him put a great axe (Roger de Hoveden calls it a Danish axe) into his hand, and his terrible strokes held the pack of his foes off for some time longer. As a contemporary source describes it: "Then was seen the might of the king, equal to a thunderbolt, slaying some with his immense axe and striking down others. Then rose the shouts afresh, all rushing against him and he against all. At last, through the number of his blows, the king's axe was broken asunder. On seeing this, William de Caimes, a most powerful knight, rushed upon the king and seizing him by the helmet cried with a loud voice, 'Here! All of you, come here. I have taken the king!'"

In a manuscript made in Bury St. Edmunds between 1121 and 1148 is a picture of an axe-wielding warrior (fig. 19) who might have been Stephen himself.

Fig. 19. Knight wielding a "Danish" axe

The axe of the horseman was gen-erally a small, light weapon easily wielded in one hand, but we do sometimes see the great two-handed "Danish" axe in action on horseback.

The little horseman's axes varied a good deal during the medieval period, showing many changes that may be attributed to the places they were made in, like the bill-hooks. But as the centuries passed, the edge of the axe tended to become straight rather than curved (fig. 20). At the

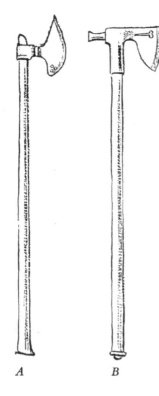

A   *B*

Fig. 20. Horseman's axes.
A, c. 1200; B, c. 1400

end of the period, during the late fifteenth and early sixteenth centuries, axes became small and narrow and often had either a hammer head or a pick on the back of the head (fig. 21).

During the fourteenth century another type of axe came into use. It was for fighting on foot, but it was no infantryman's weapon. It was, instead, a knightly adaptation of one. It is called a poll-axe, which describes it well, for it is an axe for smashing "polls" or heads. The top of the

Fig. 21. Horseman's axe, c. 1510

weapon, often of most admirable workmanship, is like a halberd head or a pick, and there is a long spearlike spike in front. These poll-axes varied a good deal. Some had straight edges, others curved. The hammer head might have a flat or a slightly ridged face, or it might have six great teeth, the same shape as the spikes in cricket boots (fig. 22). In some poll-axes the haft is quite short, only about four feet, but in others it may be six feet. It was not until the middle years of the fifteenth century that this weapon became really popular with the knightly classes; but between about 1430 and 1530 it

Fig. 22. Poll-axe head, c. 1450

was in favor, particularly in single combat on foot. Many of these fights took place in tournaments, or as duels over points of honor, but during this period they often were fought to settle judicial matters, a late development of the old "trial by combat." They were fought, whether to settle affairs of honor or points of law, in a small, square, fenced-off enclosure about the size of a boxing ring, called the *champ clos.* The contestants usually wore full armor, but it was a matter of choice. Many famous duels were fought in this way.

The method of fighting with these long poll-axes and poll-hammers was simple and effective (fig. 23). You had the axe on one side to cut at your opponent with, a hammer or a spike on the other to

Fig. 23. Fighting with poll-axes

hit him with, and a long spike in the head so that you could thrust like a spear. The weapon was held by both hands grasping the haft, widely spaced to give the most power to your blows, speed to your movements, and strength to your parries. One hand held it some eighteen inches below the head. This leading hand was often protected by a roundel on the haft, like the vamplate on a lance, but the other hand was generally left unguarded, since it was out of the danger area of the weapon. You could parry with these things as you would with a quarter-staff, or our old friend the rifle with fixed bayonet. Your blows would be made fairly slowly – indeed, all the movements of fighting with these weapons must have been slow and rather ponderous.

The same sort of method was used with the halberd and the bill. The latter was a most excellent weapon, for in spite of its greater length, its head was much lighter than the poll-axe and the halberd. All those hooks and spikes and lugs were useful in defense and deadly when attacking on foot. Armed with a bill, and provided you were quick and nimble, you had an excellent defense against the weapons of a mounted antagonist. I have used one myself in this way during a demonstration, and it is surprising how easy it is to catch his sword or axe or mace and turn it aside with your bill; and in the same movement you can thrust the point into him, or cut at him with the edge or, back-handed, hack him with the spike.

The halberd was used like an axe, but it had one useful adjunct lacking in an axe. If an armored and mounted knight was struck on the back of his head, or between his shoulders, he would fall forward out of his saddle, exposing the unarmored parts of his thighs and seat. As the knight went forward, his opponent then could thrust at these exposed parts with the great spike on the head of the halberd. A nasty weapon. You could of course do just the same with a bill or a poll-axe.

The poll-axe (or poll-hammer) seems to have been perhaps the most popular weapon. But swords and spears, or spearlike weapons consisting simply of a steel spike about thirty inches long fastened to a four-foot haft, were also used. In tournaments, the contestants' hands were guarded by besagews, or discs of steel set on the shaft above the hand-grip like a sword-guard or the vamplate of a lance. Occasionally, ordinary cross-hilted swords were fitted with these besagews as an added protection in duels. When we read, "How a man schal be armyd at his ese when he schall fyghte on foote," we find that on occasions his sword "shall be wel besagewed afore ye hilts." We have met this particular set of knightly instructions before, in dealing with armor, and we shall see more of it when we discuss knights' swords in the next chapter.

The war-hammer was similar in use to the axe; the head was quite large, generally about three inches long by two inches square, with a toothed face and a long, stout pick balancing it at the back. The haft was usually about 2 to 2½ feet long, sometimes quite plain like an axe-haft, sometimes with a sort of hilt at the end, bound with wire and leather thonging, with a small besagew in front of

Fig. 24. War-hammer, c. 1420

the hand and a little sort of rudimentary pommel at the end, but these were rare (fig. 24). More common was the plain wooden or steel haft. Enormously popular during the second half of the fifteenth century was the poll-hammer, a similar though larger head set on a long haft, like a poll-axe, and used in the same way (fig. 25).

Fig. 25. Fighting with poll-hammers

The mace, of course, started off in remote times as a club. Many fine stone maces survive, generally more or less spherical stones with a hole through the middle, but some were deadly things finely wrought into the form of a disc, also of stone. The ancient Egyptians were fond of these, and

large numbers survive. There are many bronze mace-heads, too, but on the whole it is not possible

Fig. 26. Bronze mace-head

to be sure whether they are of the Bronze Age or the Middle Ages, for the shape of many bronze mace-heads was also popular between 1200 and 1500 A.D (fig. 26). But it is quite possible that mace-heads made in, say, 800 B.C. and A.D. 1300 were identical in form and material. Even so, there are shapes that seem to belong exclusively to one period, and many of them are knightly weapons. One of these, found in London (fig. 27), is typical of many shown on monumental sculptures and manuscript pictures of a period between about 1230 and 1350.

During the later fifteenth century maces became shapely weapons. In fact, from about 1440 to 1510 most weapons were not only very beautiful in form – more so than they had ever been before and would ever be again – but were most magnificently made. The art of the armorer and the weaponsmith most certainly reached its peak at this time. The mace of this

Fig. 27. Iron mace, c. 1300, found in London (London Museum)

period was a small weapon with a flanged head; the flanges were acutely pointed, in contrast to the flatter forms of the earlier types (fig. 28). This shape, however, seems to have had its disadvantages: instead of merely denting and crushing armor, its sharp flanges tended to punch through it, causing the mace to get completely stuck and so become wrenched from its owner's hand. By the early years of the sixteenth century the flanges of mace-heads became flatter again, but much more ornamental than before (fig. 29); they got bigger too. The small, light mace with its sharp flanges, weighing about 2½ pounds, was only in use between about 1465 and 1490; both before and after, it had flatter flanges and weighed between four and six pounds.

Sometimes – particularly before 1450 – the shafts of

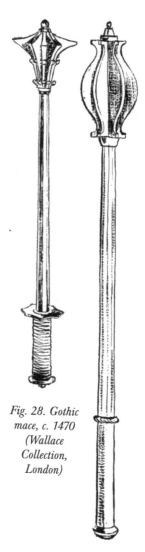

Fig. 28. Gothic mace, c. 1470 (Wallace Collection, London)

Fig. 29. Mace, 16th century

maces were of wood, but after 1450 they were elaborately made of steel.

One form of mace constantly seen in the illustrations to historical stories, as well as in drawings of knights, is a round ball with masses of great spikes sticking out of it. Though such mace-heads survive, they are crude things; like those ball-and-chain weapons – three spiked balls each on a length of chain fastened to the end of a pole – the spiked-ball mace was an infantry weapon. Beastly things they were, but given lovely names: the macelike thing was called a Morning Star, and the ball-and-chain affair was called a Holy Water Sprinkler. Our ancestors had a certain grim humor in naming some of their less gentlemanly weapons.

Sword and Dagger

The sword of chivalry is a familiar but completely misunderstood object. How many illustrations are there, I wonder, to historical stories, where the swords shown are ridiculous as well as inaccurate? A medieval sword has three main elements or parts: the blade, the cross-guard, and the pommel. This pommel, a large knob on top of the hilt, gives proper balance to the blade and is, in effect, simply a weight put there as a counterpoise to the weight of the blade. Without an adequate pommel, a sword is as unbalanced as a conventionally designed airplane would be without a tail-plane, and as unmanageable as the same aircraft would be if it had no rudder. To the craftsmen who made swords, too, the weapon was an object of beauty and good design; the proportions had to be right. So the pommel was always big enough to look good. Figure 30 gives you an idea of the proper proportions of a sword of this period of chivalry.

There were a great many variations in the shapes of blade, cross, and pommel between the years 1100 and 1500, but the basic design was the same throughout.

It is often said that these swords were heavy and clumsy and almost impossible to handle, but this is not so. The average weight was less than three pounds, and, as I have said, each weapon was balanced in such a way that it was easy to handle. Mind you, to a modern person, even three pounds of sword seems an awful lot to have to wield for hours on end, especially with the force needed in a fight. But remember that these warriors were trained to use such weapons from the age of about ten; every day a boy of the proper class would practice with a sword. Not, naturally, a full-sized three-pounder, but a small one made to suit his strength. As he grew, he used larger and heavier weapons.

Fig. 30. How a 15th-century sword should look

In this way, the muscles of arm, shoulder, and back became very strong, and by the time a boy became a full-fledged fighter (usually when he was about 15) he would be quite powerful enough to manage any sort of full-sized weapon.

In most museums one may see one or two medieval swords. Nearly all of these have been dug out of river beds and fields, and are blackened, corroded, and rather pathetic objects, looking as if they were crudely made out of iron bars. No doubt you have seen, in tidal estuaries and creeks near coastlines, the hulks of boats rotting in the mud, their blackened ribs sticking dismally out at low tide. And as you look at them, you know that they were once proud sailing craft, with all the swift grace and beauty of their kind. The blackened remains of swords are similar; they are as far from the gleaming, deadly beauty of "living" swords as the rotting hulk is from the loveliness of a new yacht. One tends to think the only surviving swords from the centuries between 1100 and 1500 are these relics, but it is not so, luckily. There are many knightly swords that seem hardly to have felt the hand of time; their blades are as fresh and sharp as ever, and their hilts retain their wood and leather grips, still bearing the impress of the hard grasp of the warrior's hand. Many such swords are in private collections, but many may be seen in museums throughout Europe and America.

In illustrating this chapter, I shall show several swords of this kind, some of which you should be able to go and see.

A good many swords come between these two extremes. They have been buried deep in the soft mud of rivers, completely cut off from the destructive effects of oxygen. Their blades are black, but retain their original shape almost intact. The blackness is a chemical deposit of iron that completely preserves the steel underneath. Several swords preserved in this way may be seen in the armories of the Tower of London, as well as a few medieval ones that have never been lost or buried, but always kept clean and cared for. In its original state, the blade of a medieval sword (as of any other) would have been burnished like a mirror.

The size of these weapons varied a good deal, much as the size of the men who wielded them varied. Some are quite small and light, some are quite big and heavy. There are, however, two kinds of sword which are bigger than normal. One kind used to be called a "war sword" and the other, as you may expect, was called the "two-hand sword." During the thirteenth century and the early part of the fourteenth, the war sword was a big weapon, though not as big as a real two-hander; it was, nevertheless, wielded in either both hands or in just one (fig. 31D). Its average length was thirty-eight inches in the blade and seven inches in the grip.

The true two-hander was the same shape as the ordinary sword, but a great deal bigger; its average size was about fifty inches in the blade and twelve inches in the grip, giving a total length of around five feet. It was not until the sixteenth century that the typical two-hand sword made its appearance, with its very long, curved cross-guard and the sharp lugs sticking out of each side of the blade below the hilt. The medieval one was just an exceptionally big sword of ordinary shape.

The war sword was, as its name implies, not carried about on everyday occasions, but was reserved for the field of battle. It was essentially a horseman's weapon, since a long sword was generally needed when fighting on horseback. With such a sword a fighter could be sure of reaching his opponent without having to get very close to him. The average weight of such swords was about 4½ to 5 pounds.

During the second half of the fourteenth century, long, rather heavy swords (not war swords) became popular. They had seven-inch long grips and have been called "hand-and-a-half swords" because they could be used in either one hand or in two. Many are shown on monuments.

Though some of the variations in the sizes of swords occurred simply because they were made for big or small men, there were two basic different sizes with which a knight fought in different ways.

Consider, especially, what happened during the fifteenth century. The long sword I have just mentioned, with its grip long enough to use in both hands yet light enough for one hand, became distinct after about 1420 from the short sword or "arming sword." Often on horseback the knight would wear two swords: his arming sword at his own belt, and his long sword fastened to the front of his saddle. When he fought on foot in the lists, either to engage in a judicial duel or a friendly fight called a "just of pees" or "joust of peace," or in an affair of honor, he often took two swords with him.

Here is what was said concerning this point in a manuscript written about 1450, setting forth "how a man schal be armyd at his ese." After describing in detail the sort of garments worn under armor, it goes on to say how such a man should be armed:

> To arme a man. Ffirste ye muste sette on Sabatones and tye hem up on the shoo with smale poyntis that woll not breke. And then griffus [greaves] and then cuisses and ye breche of mayle. And the Tonletis [tonlet – sometimes called the fauld – overlapping hoops of plate to protect the abdomen below the waist]. And the Brest and ye Vambras and ye rerebras [armor for the arms and shoulders] and then gloovis. And then hang his daggere up on his right side. And then his shorte sworde on his lyfte side in a rounde rynge all nakid to pulle it out lightli. And then putte his cote upon his back. And

then his basinet pyind [pinned-fastened] up on
two greet staplis before the breste with a dow-
bill bokill [double buckle] behynde up on the
bak for to make the basinet sitte juste. And
then his longe swerd in his hande. And then his
pensil [pennon] in his hande peynted of St.
George or of oure Ladye to bless him with as
he goeth towarde the felde and in the felde.

Sometimes a knight took other weapons – axe,
mace, hammer, poll-axe, or poll-hammer –
instead of his "long swerd." It is interesting –
indeed, it is a most vital bit of information – that he
had his short sword in a round ring, unsheathed so
he could pull it out lightly. One often wonders
what the warrior did with his scabbard when he
fought on foot. Try fighting in a demonstration on
stage with a scabbard attached from your waist and
you will know what a menace it can be. What they
do on stage is what they did in the lists and probably in battle – wear the sword unsheathed, just a
ring around it, no scabbard.

We don't know a great deal about the methods
used when fighting with swords in any period
before about 1550, when the art of fencing began
to develop. That sword-fighting needed skill, training, and knowledge there can be no doubt, but in
the earlier days of the Age of Chivalry, knights
must have used swords much as their Viking predecessors did. These tremendous fighters have left

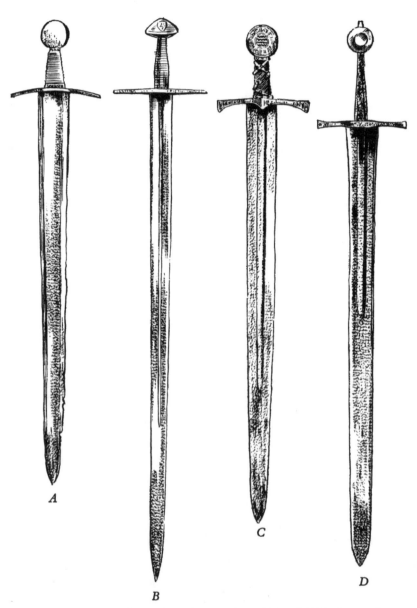

Fig. 31. Eight sword types dating between about 1050 and 1450, showing the changes in hilt and blade forms. A, c. 1050. Musée de l'armée, Paris; B. c. 1150. Kunstistoriches Museum, Vienna; C. c. 1250. Instituto del Conde de Valencia, Madrid; D. c. 1300. Armouries of the Tower of London

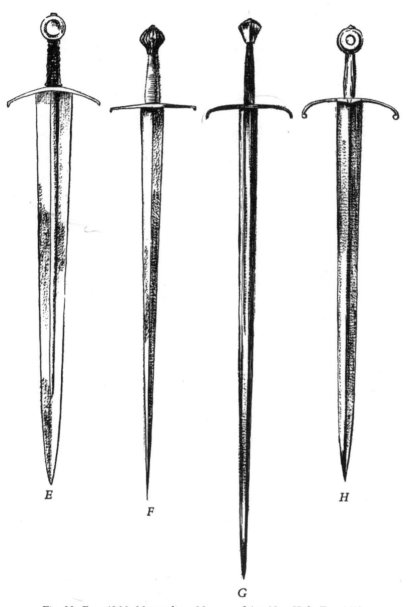

Fig. 32. E. c. 1300. Metropolitan Museum of Art, New York; F. c. 1413.
Treasury of the Cathedral at Monza (the sword of Estre Visconti, killed in 1413);
G. c. 1380. Fitzwilliam Museum, Cambridge; H. c. 1420. The sword of King
Henry V, The Library, Westminster Abbey

behind a good deal of information about their sword-play in their stories and poems. It is quite clear from these sources that it was not a simple matter of sword clashing against sword in the dashing and attractive manner of Robin Hood on television or in the movies. For one thing, the sword was rarely if ever used for parrying. A knight carried a shield on the left arm for that – either he parried his opponent's blow with his shield, or he leaped and ducked out of its way. A good swordsman, like a good boxer, had to be very nimble on his feet, and his reactions needed to be lightning swift: often the only way to avoid a great downward slash that could take off a knight's shoulder and arm, even if he had a mail shirt on, was to move sideways away from it, either by leaping aside, or twisting sideways from the hips – quicker to do – or bending sideways. A favorite blow was a sweeping slash at the knees, and the only way to avoid this blow was to jump over it; there would be no time to parry with your shield; and generally it came as a backhanded stroke at the right knee, away from the shield.

In the old slashing, smashing days of mail armor and broad, flat-bladed cutting swords, the wrist was little used in sword-fighting. A blow was made from the shoulder, the arm straight and the sword a rigid, yet sensitive and flexible, extension of it. There were two possible reasons for this: it provided a more effective and powerful slash; and if a medieval knight wore a long mail sleeve, he would soon tire if he continually flexed his elbows with the mail rolling up in the bend of it. If you move your elbow with just a jersey on, you'll see how the cloth of the sleeve wrinkles and folds together inside the bend of your elbow; then imagine what a medieval knight would have had to go through wearing hard rings of mail.

These knightly swords were capable of doing a great deal of damage. They were made of enormously hard steel – you can't even scratch an old one with a modern file – and their edges were literally kept as sharp as razors. When such a weapon was swung by a powerful arm and shoulder, which had developed enormous strength from a lifetime of practice, we need not be surprised when we read how, in medieval times, arms and legs and heads were chopped off even though they were armored in mail. There is plenty of reference to such events in the writings of the time, not simply in songs and poems, which may pardonably exaggerate a little, but in sober chronicles written by clerks concerned only with recording what happened, not with making the most of a good tale.

Even more to the point, perhaps, are the things we know from experience, of what the Japanese could do with their single-edged swords. The Japanese Samurai warrior was remarkably like the medieval knight, and, unlike that remote person, only ceased to exist as a fighting unit in his full medieval panoply of armor about 130 years ago. His warrior-code, his strength of arm and skill in swordsmanship, and his sword were still in use in World War II. We know the Samurai warrior could cut a man in half with a single sideways blow, and take his head off with ease and very neatly. He could cleave his body in two diagonally from the shoulder to the opposite hip, and split him down the middle from the crown of his head to his hips. One method of testing a new blade was to cut a man in half across the hips. This was done across a block, for you had to shear through his spine, hip bones, and pelvis – a lot of bone to get through in one blow. Such tests were carried out upon condemned criminals. Knowing that this could be done by the Japanese, we need not in the least doubt that medieval European warriors could do the same.

When the great change in arming came about in the second half of the fourteenth century, it became necessary to use the sword for thrusting; you could bang away at a man in plate armor with the edge of your sword and your blows would only glance off, but a powerful and well-directed thrust might penetrate the little gaps which even the best-designed plate armor couldn't cover. Because of this, as I have said, after the 1350s most swords were made with narrow, stiff, and very sharply pointed blades. Later, during the fifteenth century, armor became very expensive, so it was not extensively used. (A good, strong, well-designed, ordinary armor, without embellishment and mass-produced, cost what by modern standards would be about $15,000 – the price of a small car. Armor made by a master, the equivalent of a Rolls or a Jaguar, could cost as much as one of those cars.) Poor knights and men-at-arms and ordinary troopers had to make do with only partial plate armor or go back to wearing mail. So swords became useful again. A style of sword that was perfect for a cut-and-thrust type of fighting was designed – it was sharply pointed, with a broad blade stiffened by a ridge running down the middle from hilt to point. Figure 32H is a good example. Many of these swords still exist, and they are the loveliest weapons, both to look at and to handle, ever to have been made. They are light, averaging 2½ pounds, and are beautifully balanced. To hold one can be a curious experience, making the arm tingle as you feel the wonder of the weapon.

By the time these swords were made, the shield had been abandoned by the fully armored knight. It was an unnecessary encumbrance since armor alone was adequate protection. Even so, partially armored men and foot-fighters still used shields, often little circular bucklers; but the sword, it became evident, could often by itself provide sufficient defense. The great snag in using the sword for parrying, however, was that its edge tended to get badly cut about. One would imagine that it would be much better always to turn the blade a little and parry with the flat of it, but such was physically impractical. The wrist, if turned so that the flat of the blade opposed a blow, would be in an unnatural position and unable to resist the blow strongly enough; by contrast, if the sword's edge opposed the blow, one's wrist would be set at a more natural angle to the arm so that all the strength of the muscles could be utilized to hold the blade steady; the other way, the opposing blow would bend one's hand easily, with the sword in it.

During the fifteenth century the problem of single-handed sword fighting was studied and theorized; numerous "fight books" were produced, full of lively drawings showing how to use weapons (fig. 33). Much of the sword-play still involved acrobatics; though one parried with a sword, one still had to dodge and duck and leap about as much as ever. There was a good deal of wrestling, too. A knight would grab his opponent's sword-hand, lock his own sword-arm around his foe's neck, and dig the pommel into the opponent's ear; a knight would then hook the cross of his hilt under his knee to bring his foe down. Often a knight would turn his sword around, close in and strike at his foe's face with the pommel – the

Fig. 33. Adapted from Talhoffer's "Fechtbuch" of 1467, fighting with the long sword:
(from top) Parrying a slash on the left side. Disarming. A surprise move: reversing the
sword and using the pommel. One way of dealing with your opponent

phrase *to pommel* or *to pummel* comes from this sort of action. Sometimes a knight had a little buckler in his left hand to help him parry, while other times he had a dagger; still other times a knight might wrap a cloth around his arm.

This art of fighting seems to have been most fully developed in Spain, where by the 1460s additional guards had been added to the hilt to protect fingers from an opponent's blade (fig. 57). In Spain, too, we find the origin of the well-known word *rapier*. During the Middle Ages it was not customary to wear a sword in ordinary civil dress; you only wore it with armor. But at the end of this period, especially in Spain, the new art of fencing made it sensible to wear the sword even without armor. By the 1470s we find a new expression in Spanish writing, "espada de ropera," which means literally "costume sword," a sword worn with ordinary dress. The French took the word *ropera* – as well as the fashion of wearing a sword – and called it *rapiere*. The custom spread to England, where the word became *rapier*.

In German-speaking lands a thrusting sword had always been called *degen*, meaning simply a thrusting sword, and they never used the Spanish-originated word *rapier*.

If a knight fought a formal duel at any time in the Middle Ages, he tended to fight lance to lance, sword to sword, axe to axe, and so on. But in battle it was very different. He might find his sword opposed to a mace or a poll-axe or anything else. He might even find his only weapon to be a dagger. So in training a man-at-arms, it was necessary to ensure that he knew exactly how to handle all these different weapons, and how to oppose each one with every other.

There was, as I said, much variation in the shape of swords during the Age of Chivalry, but the differences were slight and subtle. The best way to show them in a book is to draw them, as in Figures 31 and 32. I have shown some of the best surviving swords of different periods. All of these actual swords are in good, fresh condition – some, indeed, look as if they were used only about last week, they are so fine. You can see some of the different forms of pommel and cross-guard, and – if you look carefully – you can see differences in the shape of blades. Of course, many of these types were in use during the same time period, though I have selected ones which can be dated with some accuracy to within half a century or so. The active life of one of these swords was long; it might well be over a hundred years; so even if we say it was probably made about 1350, it may still have been used in 1440. This makes determining the exact historical use of some swords a bit difficult. Keep in mind: when in a museum or in an illustration in a book you see a weapon labeled "sword, possibly

Italian, 1410-40," you can be pretty sure it was made sometime between those two dates; but the dating implies nothing much about its active life. Some medieval swords, as well as armor, were probably brought out of private armories to fight with during the great English Civil War of 1642-49.

Sword-blades often had inscriptions inlaid in them. There were various methods of doing this, and at different times varying styles of inscription were used. During the Age of the Vikings it was customary to inlay on one side of the blade a series of marks that, though incomprehensible to us, were meaningful to the Vikings; on the other side of the blade was the name of the bladesmith who made it. Figure 34 shows some of these names and marks, which were all made by inlaying letters of iron into the steel of the blade. The smith would cut his letter-

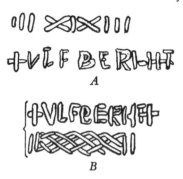

Fig. 34. A and B. Names and marks inlaid in iron on the blades of Viking swords. (The name goes on one side, the pattern on the other.) c. 900

Fig. 34C. Here the name is on one side, and a Latin phrase "Man of God" on the other. c. 1100

ing or marks with a cold chisel, probably when the blade was hot. Then he would take little lengths of iron rod, usually twisted, heat his blade and his bits of rod to welding heat, and hammer the rods into the slots he had cut. Then, after cooling and tempering, the whole thing would be burnished. At this stage, the letters would be quite invisible, so the blade was probably lightly etched with a mild acid so that the letters showed. I have one of these swords, made by the Ingelri workshop, where all the letters have survived in a perfectly preserved blade. When it is polished, no inscription is visible, but if it is etched the letters show quite clearly.

At the end of the Viking period, particularly in swords made for Christians, the pagan symbols on the reverse of the blade were replaced by more Christian symbols: the words *In Nomine Domini* (in the name of the Lord). But until about 1050, they were still mostly inlaid in iron. Some blades of the Vikings' time were inlaid in much smaller letters of silver, tin, or copper, and after about 1100 this method became usual and the old

D

Fig. 34D. Here the name is followed by the words "Me Fecit," meaning "Gicelin Made Me," and on the reverse "In the name of The Lord"

iron inlays went out of fashion.

The later forms of inlay were made in much the same way as the earlier ones, but the actual letters and marks were made by insetting short bits of wire – silver, tin, or copper, or a type of brass called latten – into the marked-out slots in the blade. In these cases, the marks would almost certainly have been hammered in while the blade was cold (fig. 35).

Some blades of this 1125-1225 period have just

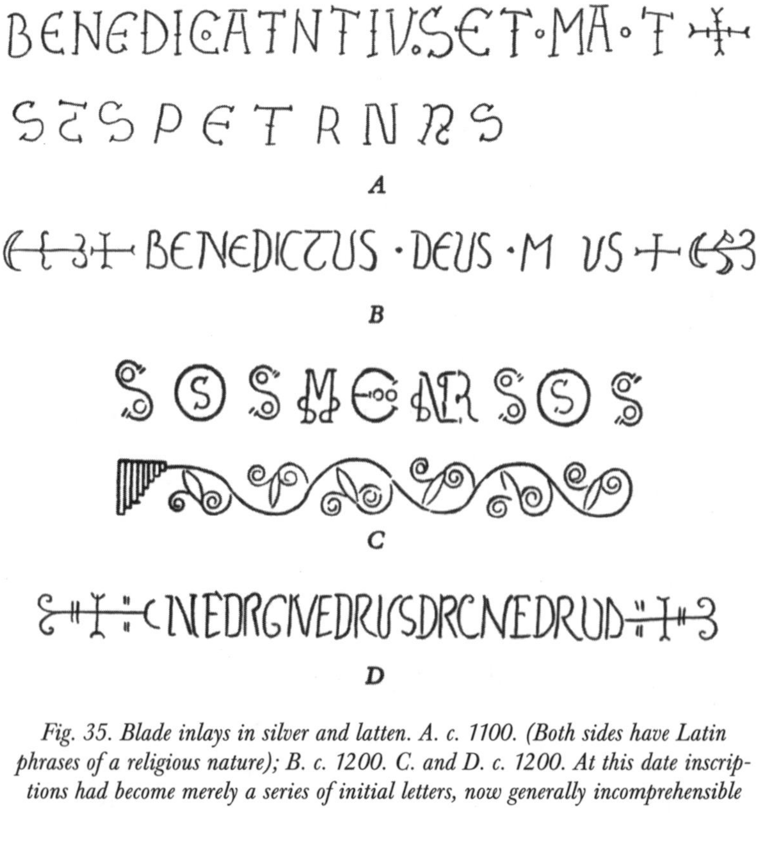

BENEDICATNTIVSET·MA·T ⁜

SƐS P Ɛ T R N ßS

A

⟨⟨⟨-3-I- BENEDICZUS ·DEUS ·M US +⟨⟨53

B

S ⊙ S ⅏Ɛ⅍ S⊙ S
⫛⟿⟿⟿⟿

C

&·⟨I⟨ CNEDRGNEDRISDRCNEDRUD⟨I⟨3

D

Fig. 35. Blade inlays in silver and latten. A. c. 1100. (Both sides have Latin phrases of a religious nature); B. c. 1200. C. and D. c. 1200. At this date inscriptions had become merely a series of initial letters, now generally incomprehensible

a few simple marks, such as a cross within a circle, often several times repeated, or an S within a circle, or a simple, very small inscription, OSO or SOS. This, we believe, stands for O Sancta (O Blessed) as does the encircled S.

From the second half of the thirteenth century until early in the fourteenth, say from 1250 until 1310, the letters of the inscription were placed so close together as to be almost unintelligible, forming a pattern of upright lines along the fuller of the blade. (The fuller, by the way, is that channel which runs down from the hilt, often nearly as far as the point. Often called a "blood-channel," it has nothing whatever to do with blood. The sole purpose was to lighten and strengthen the blade.)

After about 1310, inscriptions became simpler, often consisting of only four letters, widely spread out along the blade. About this time, too – probably a bit earlier, say about 1280 – smiths' marks reappeared. Not names, but just marks, like trademarks (which of course they were). Sometimes these were inlaid in latten or silver, and sometimes they were made with a punch (fig. 36 shows some of each kind). During the second half of the fourteenth century and the first half of the fifteenth, inscriptions disappeared from blades altogether, but were often found on hilts instead. Marks, however, were very frequent, though after 1450 inscriptions on blades made a comeback.

Fig. 36. Smiths' marks

The reason inscriptions on blades went out of fashion after about 1325 is this: a radical change in the shape of blades came about. During all of the migration and Viking periods (from about A.D. 300 until about 1300), the section of sword blades was always flat and thin with a broad central fuller (fig. 37A). These were purely cutting and slashing weapons. Early in the fourteenth century, in certain specialized swords made for thrusting, the section of the blade was like a flattened diamond (fig. 37B). When the great changeover in the fashion and make of armor came about in the 1350s, and a complete and more-or-less impenetrable plate replaced the old-style mail, the old flat cutting sword became far less effective than it had been, so a new type of stiff, acutely pointed thrusting sword came in. These swords were either of the flattened diamond section or of a flat hexagonal section (fig. 38). In most of these

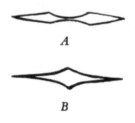

Fig. 37. Blade cross sections

78

swords the central part of the blade was too narrow to carry an inscription; it was not until the 1450s when the old style of flat, fullered blade came back into favor that inscriptions reappeared on blades. There were exceptions, however. Some swords with a diamond-section blade had a deep fuller cut in the upper half, with an inscription in small letters inlaid in it.

The hilts of medieval swords were generally quite plain, but a few decorated ones survive. The most common decoration appeared in the circular centers of pommels of the so-called "wheel" form (see fig. 46B). This decoration is often in the form of the arms or crest of the owner, but various devices may have been used – indeed, any device the owner may have fancied. Sometimes these decorations were enameled, sometimes simply engraved on a plate of gold, bronze-gilt, or silver inset into the metal of the pommel. Occasionally we find a pommel engraved with running designs of foliage – this too seems mostly to have been applied to the wheel-form pommels. Similar decoration

Fig. 38. Blade cross section

sometimes appears on cross-guards, but far more rarely. It is a curious thing about medieval sword-hilts that often a pommel may be decorated – gilded, silver-plated, engraved, or inlaid – while the cross of the same sword is of perfectly plain iron.

Fig. 39. Viking sax, c. 850

Fig. 40. 13th-century falchion. (The library, Durham Cathedral)

The before-mentioned facts pertain to the straight, two-edged sword; but there was another kind with a curved blade that was used all through the Middle Ages. This type, called the falchion, was mainly a weapon of the infantryman, but on occasions was used by the knights. This weapon was a direct descendant of a useful little weapon much favored by the Vikings, called a sax. Generally shorter than the long sword, it had one curved cutting edge and a "back" – that is, the other edge was squared off and straight, while the cutting edge curved to meet it in a sharp point, just like an enormous kitchen knife (fig. 39). Though some medieval falchions were similar to such a knife (fig. 40), others, stemming from an Eastern European type, were like a modern saber. (This latter look is best typified by a splendid example that belonged to Charlemagne in the eighth century – see fig. 41). In nearly all cases the cutting edge was convex, but there are examples (of the Viking saxes too) where it was concave, giving a rather strange look to the weapon (fig. 42).

The hilts of these falchions were similar to ordinary sword-hilts until the fifteenth century, when they began to be furnished with an extra guard for the hand in addition to the plain cross. This guard, a bar branching off one arm of the cross and curving up toward the pommel, protected the knuckles.

To complete a sword, to turn its basic ironwork into a practical weapon, a grip is needed. This part, as its name implies, is what you hold the sword by, placed between the cross and the pommel. The grip is made of wood, variously covered by

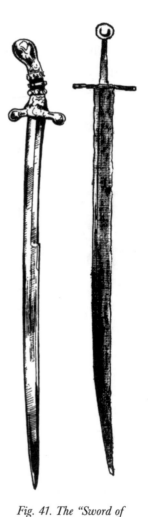

Fig. 41. The "Sword of Charlemagne," c. 850. Waffensammlung, Vienna Fig. 42. Falchion, c. 1250, with concave edge. (Collection of Mr. Harold Peterson, Arlington, Virginia)

binding with cord or wire, or with leather, parchment, linen, or velvet; many different fabrics were used. These grips were often very decorative, especially in the thirteenth and fourteenth centuries.

Often the wooden core would be bound with a fine cord of, say, yellow silk; over this, made in the manner of a string-bag, would be a binding of thicker scarlet cord. The whole grip might be finished with a sort of tassel at top and bottom (fig. 43). Or a binding of silver wire might be "string-bagged" with a cord of green silk. Sometimes, instead of a tassel, the lower part of a grip might be finished with a chappe, a sort of double flap falling in a semicircle over either side of the central part of the cross-guard (fig. 44). Often these chappes – a word, incidentally, that means "capes" – were decorated in needlework with the arms or device of the owner.

Fig. 43. The sword of Fernando de la Cerda, a prince of Castile who died in 1270. From his tomb in Burgos

Of course, these "soft" fittings must have been replaced often, or at least re-covered. It is likely that the hard core outlasted a sword's working life, but the bindings, tassels, and chappes must have worn out quite quickly – not to mention the strong likelihood that they might have been stained with blood.

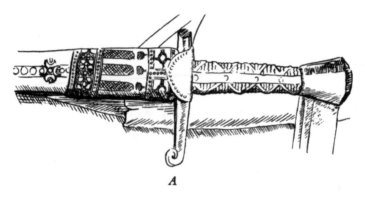

Fig. 44A. The "chappe" on a sword hilt covering the mouth of the
scabbard, from the tomb of sir John Wyard, who died in 1411

The way a complete sword was assembled,
how the hilt was fastened immovably to the blade,
is of especial interest. In brief, this is how it was
done: every blade was finished with a long "tang"
or tongue, a narrow piece at the top. The cross
was pierced in the center with a slot, through
which the tang would pass.
Similarly, the pommel had a
hole bored through it from
top to bottom, through
which the top end of the
tang went, leaving about a
quarter of an inch protruding. This protruding end was
then treated as a rivet and
hammered over until the
whole thing was secure. But

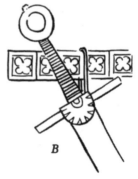

Fig. 44B. From a Bohemian
manuscript, c. 1380

83

what about the grip in the middle? Well, there were two ways of fitting a grip. In swords of the Viking period, and until about 1250, the tang was broad and flat. The wooden core of the grip was made by forming a sort of sandwich. A flat piece of wood, shaped as required, was fitted to either side of the flat tang. Each bit was hollowed out on the inside to accommodate the tang and the edges were glued together; the whole thing was securely covered and bound up, then the pommel was put on and the rivet hammered firmly down. But after about 1250 most tangs were narrow, like stalks, and a different technique was used, a simple one. The grip was carved, solid, to the required shape. Then a hole was bored from end to end. Then the tang itself was heated up; the grip was held firmly in a vice, and the hot tang bored its own hole in its own grip. In this way, a perfect fit was assured. We know this method was used because in many grips surviving from later periods, and a few from the Middle Ages that have been examined when separated from their swords, we can see the marks of the burning-out on the inside of the grip and can observe the perfect fit. It was also the only easy way to do the job, and so was obviously the right one. Since I make swords as well as write about and draw them, I speak from practical experience too.

When a grip is bored, it can be covered and

bound; then it is placed in position, firmly wedged if wedging is needed, the pommel put on top and the tang riveted over. This is shown in Figure 45.

In everyday situations, swords were worn with or carried in a scabbard. In the Middle Ages scabbards were made in exactly the same way as in the Bronze Age or the eighteenth century. The blade itself – every individual blade – was a "former" for its scabbard. Two very thin slats of wood were placed on either side of the blade, and shaped carefully to fit. These were covered in leather, parchment, linen, velvet – whatever one preferred – in the same manner as some grips. This cover was glued to the wood and sewn down the middle of the back or at one side. Until about 1310, no metal fitting was put at the top, only a chappe at the point end to prevent it from wearing away, but after this date there was always a metal locket as well. The locket had rings to which the belt-ends were fitted. In the earlier scabbards, belt-ends themselves were bound around the scabbard (fig. 46A and 46B).

Fig. 45. How a sword hilt was assembled

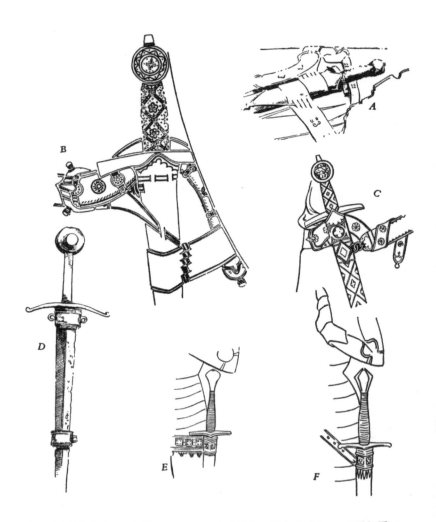

Fig. 46. Belt-fittings. A. From a monument at Halton Holgate, Lincs. c. 1300. The two ends of the wide belt are fitted to the top of the scabbard; B. From the brass of Sir Robert de Bures, Acton, Suffolk. 1302. A variation of the same arrangement; C. From the brass of Sir Robert de Septrans, Chartham, Kent. 1306. Here there is a metal locket for the lower belt-end; D. A sword, c. 1325, found in the Thames (London Museum). Here two lockets of silver take the belt-ends; E. From the brass of Sir John Peyrent, Digswell, Herts., 1415. A single metal locket is fitted at the back with very short straps attached to a horizontal belt worn round the hips; F. From the brass of Sir John de Harpeyden, c. 1430, Westminster Abbey. A small metal locket takes the ends of a diagonally worn belt in rings at the back

Lockets varied in shape depending on the period in which they were made. Figure 46 shows this progressive change of fashion, and, moreover, illustrates that until about 1430, the top of the scabbard formed two triangles overlapping each side of the central part of the cross; but in later weapons, keep in mind that this ecusson, as the center of a cross-guard is called, came down to a cusped point that fit into a similarly shaped space in the locket. There were, of course, exceptions; crosses had cusped ecussons before 1430, and scabbards overlapped upwards after, but these exceptions seem to have been very rare.

Quite often swords, in battle, were loosely fastened to the warrior. In some cases a ring was around the grip, loose so that it could run up and down freely. A light chain about three feet, six inches long was attached to the ring. The other end of the chain was fastened to the breastplate, so if your sword got knocked out of your hand, you didn't lose it. Another method was to wear a sword-knot, a loop of leather thong or similar material that was fixed to the sword-hilt and slipped over the wrist. Jean Froissart, a chronicler of the period and a contemporary of Chaucer, relates a rather amusing incident when a knight got himself into serious difficulties because of his sword-knot:

> The lords dismounted and approached the barriers, which were very strong, sword in

hand, and great strokes were given to those
within, who defended themselves very valiant-
ly. The Abbot did not spare himself, but, having
a good leather jerkin on, dealt about his blows
manfully, and received as good in his turn.
Many a gallant action was performed, and
those within the barriers flung upon the
assailants stones, logs, and pots full of lime, to
annoy them.

It chanced that Sir Henry of Flanders, who
was one of the foremost, with his sword attached
to his wrist, laid about him at a great rate; he
came too near the Abbot, who caught hold of
his sword and drew him to the barrier with so
much force that his arm was dragged through
the grating, for he could not quit his sword with
honor. The Abbot continued pulling, and had
the grating been wide enough he would have
had him through, for his shoulder had passed, to
the knight's great discomfort. On the other side,
his brother knights were trying to pull him back;
and this lasted so long that Sir Henry was sore-
ly hurt. He was at last rescued, but his sword
remained with the Abbot. And while I was writing this book, I passed through town and the
monks showed me this sword, which was kept
there, much ornamented.

Though many knights preferred to use an axe
or a mace in battle, the sword was the special arm
of knighthood. Very efficient as a weapon if used
properly, it was also symbolic of all the high ideals

and aspirations of chivalry. It was, as it were, a badge of rank.

For more than 2,000 years it had been an emblem of power and chieftainship when, in about A.D. 1100, the coming of chivalry brought the greatest glory to the sword. To its ancient traditions of power was added the final touch of Christian sanctity. The shape the sword had developed during the age of the Vikings, with its hilt like a cross, was adopted by the Church. It became protection against evil and a reminder to the sword's owner that the weapon must be used well to defend Mother Church and confuse her enemies. The sword's two-edged blade stood for loyalty and truth, one to be used against strong men who persecute the weak and the other against rich oppressors of the poor.

Knighthood was a discipline never relaxed through life, its object to make a man completely free in himself, yet obedient to the rules of knightly conduct. In the ceremonies conferring knighthood, everything was symbolic – actions, arms, and dress. The ancient ceremonial was simple – indeed, it was primeval. We speak loosely today of "dubbing" a knight, but that is a linguistic corruption of the old word *adoubement*, meaning the giving of the *adoubs*, the groups of arms that make up a warrior's equipment. This was the core of the ceremony, and the giving of the sword was the central act.

Of course, the full ceremonial was not always followed. It was the ambition of every young squire to receive his knighthood on the field of battle. When this happened, the "colee" or accolade was all that was needed, given either by his lord or captain. At the battle of Marignano (in Northern Italy) in 1515, the young King Francis I of France was knighted by that most splendid of knights, the chevalier Pierre de Terrail, known as Bayard.

It is not always safe to assume that the dagger was a short version of the sword. Medieval daggers had many and various forms, but on the whole there were only two kinds of blades. One was the true dagger-blade, sharply tapering and double-edged, and the other was the knife-blade, with one edge, often curved, and a "back" (fig.47). Until the fourteenth century, knights rarely wore daggers with their war-gear. Though we read of them *using* daggers – and sometimes in the manuscript pictures we see them using daggers – it was not until about 1290 that we see them *wearing* daggers. Where they put them is a complete puzzle. But from 1300 onwards we see daggers very often hanging from knights'

Fig. 47. 13th-century dagger

90

belts, over the right hip.

The earlier dagger (from about 1000-1150) seems to have been a knife for the most part; it was generally called cultellus, a word from which our own word cutlass comes. We know it refers to a dagger, for there is an entry in a statute drawn up in the reign of King William the Lion of Scotland (1165-1214) that refers to "...cultellum qui dicitur Dagger." We rarely find contemporary pictures of these early daggers, and the specimens that survive are few and in bad condition. They do seem, indeed, to have been knives, similar in shape to a modern kitchen knife.

After about 1230, though, daggers seem to have been thought more highly of, for we find them among knights' equipment, instead of being the weapon of peasants. Daggers' hilts became more shapely, some having a little down-curling cross-guard matched by a similarly shaped pommel (fig. 48) or a crescent-shaped pommel with a short straight cross. Others may have diamond-shaped or disc pommels – the variations by about 1250 became endless, all dependent

Fig. 48. 13th-century daggers

upon the personal taste of the weapon's maker and/or buyer.

During the second half of the fourteenth century, daggers had long hilts, which often (upon sculptured monuments) exactly matched the hilts of the swords worn upon the other side, though they were, of course, smaller (fig. 53A). In accounts of battles during the Hundred Years' War we often read of daggers used as missiles. As two opposing lines of dismounted knights approached each other they threw daggers, axes, and maces before coming to handstrokes.

From about 1325 until the end of the medieval period there seem to have been three basic kinds of dagger, each type showing innumerable variations. There was the basilard, often carried with civil dress, though we sometimes find it worn with armor. The blade was two-edged, sharply tapering, and generally rather broad, though there were narrow ones. This type, first used in the late thirteenth century, was extremely popular all through the fourteenth, though it is found only rarely in the fifteenth (fig. 49).

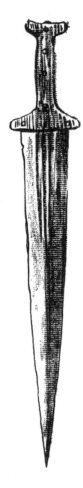

Fig. 49.
Basilard dagger

A more popular and longer-lasting kind had a distinctively shaped hilt with two kidney-like lobes at the base of the grip: it is usually referred to as the kidney dagger. This too was often worn with civil dress (carried, as all civilian daggers were in the fourteenth century, at the belt tucked in behind a large pouch or purse like a sporran), but generally the blade was back-edged, though there are many double-edged examples. This dagger type is seen on monuments dating back to the first quarter of the fourteenth century, and lasted well into the sixteenth (fig. 50). By about 1540 its shape began to change in England, developing into a typically English form of the weapon. The lobes shrank in size until they

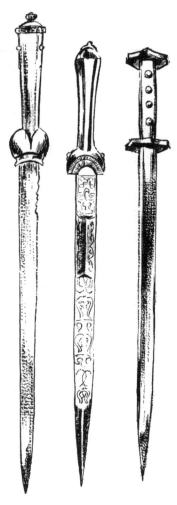

Fig. 50   Fig. 51   Fig. 52
Fig. 50. Kidney dagger, c. 1450
Fig. 51. Scottish dagger, c. 1520
Fig. 52. Rondel dagger, c. 1400

were no more than an arch between the grip and the blade. In Scotland, the same dagger developed first into a typically Scottish variant (fig. 51), and then into the well-known dirk.

A more purely military dagger was one on which both the guard and the pommel were formed of discs or roundels set at either end of the grip (fig. 52). Some of these daggers were twenty inches or more in length, almost like short swords. The blade was generally narrow and back-edged.

All through the medieval period we find daggers with ordinary pommels and cross-guards, made exactly like swords. There was infinite variety in the design of these weapons (fig. 53 shows two), but between about 1360 and 1410 there was a fashion for the short-bladed, long-hilted type with a disc-shaped pommel and a very short cross.

Fig. 53. Quillon daggers
A. c. 1380; B. c. 1450

Early Firearms

There is little connection between knights and guns, for the knight was as obsolete in the age of firearms as the hansom cab is today. But he did come into disastrous contact with gunstones and cannon-balls in his last years, so guns in their earliest forms should have a place in this book.

Various forms of fire-throwing engines had been known in ancient times, from the lump of burning fiber fastened to an arrowhead to the terrible "Greek fire" which, first used by the Byzantine Greeks and later by the Arabs, had much in common with a modern flame-thrower. It was liquid fire (oily stuff) squirted out of a tube for a considerable distance. These things, however, do not really come under the heading of "firearms," for this term only properly applies to a missile weapon which throws out a ball propelled by an explosive charge.

It now seems certain that these weapons originated in Western Europe. For quite some time it was believed the Chinese and the Arabs invented and used firearms long before Europeans, but it is now known that this mistaken idea was based entirely upon inaccurate translations from the Oriental languages. What was wrongly thought to be descriptions of guns firing shells turns out to be really descriptions of "fire works," or of pots of combustible stuff thrown by catapults. The first real gun, probably made in England, was a sort of large bottle-shaped iron pot that ejected a king-sized crossbow-bolt when the powder in the bottom of the pot was touched off. These were called *pots de fer*, and they came about as early as 1327. In the first year of the Hundred Years' War between England and France, the French fleet that raided Southampton in June 1338 was modestly furnished with one *pot de fer*, three pounds of gunpowder, and forty-eight large bolts with iron "feathers" in two boxes (fig. 54).

These weapons were small; some used by the French in defense of Cambrai in 1339 were bought by weight and the bill for the purchase gives the price of the iron by the pound. The total weight was only twenty-five pounds per gun.

In the same year we find the earliest mention of a type of gun that for some time seems to have been almost the only kind in use. It was really a nest of little guns, a series of tubes or barrels

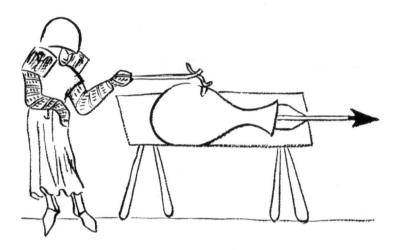

Fig. 54. Pot de Fer, 1337

clamped together with their touch-holes arranged so that a single sweep of the gunner's match would set them all off. These were called ribalds and were mounted on wheeled carts; there was a mantlet or shield for the gunner, and the whole thing was sometimes called a "cart of war." They were only effective as anti-personnel weapons, since the balls were too small to have any effect against walls. It took a terribly long time to load them, too, for each tube had to be cleaned out, charged with powder and ball, wadded, tamped down, and primed.

These ribalds soon gave way to more effective cannon. There is reasonably good evidence that some small guns were used by the English at Crecy in 1346; apart from documentary evidence, which is conflicting, a small iron ball was found on the part of the battlefield where the Genoese cross-bowmen were halted by English archers and their "three cannons." It was of about three-inch caliber, consistent with the size of the guns known to have been used in siege work in the 1340s. At various dates between 1800 and 1850 four similar balls were found roughly in the same part of the field, two of iron and two of stone.

After 1346 guns became far more common and larger, and they began to be cast in brass or copper rather than iron; in 1353 Edward III had four new guns of copper cast by William of Aldgate, a London brazier. These were still small, and though it cost only 13 shilling, 4 pence each to make them, we must remember money in the four-teenth century was worth much more than it is today. So by modern standards, we might say it would have cost around $1000 to make the guns; but consider how much it would cost to make a large gun today. That $1000 would not go very far.

By the end of the fourteenth century the size of cannon had increased further, and they were found to be most effective in battering down castle walls. But large castings tended to have flaws and air-holes in them, so another method was devised for making cannon. Around a wooden core, of the diameter required for the bore, white-hot iron bars were laid edge to edge and welded together by the blows of the gunsmith's hammer; thus the gun was made of wrought, not cast, iron. As an additional source of strength, iron rings or hoops were clamped around the outside of the gun (fig. 55).

Fig. 55. Hooped gun, c. 1420, and gunstones

Even so, there were many regrettable accidental explosions; the best known is the one that slew James II of Scotland in 1460. While his forces were besieging Roxburgh Castle, he was watching the firing of one of his big guns, a large hooped bombard made for him in Flanders and called "The Lion." Its hoops were not strong enough, for suddenly it blew up and a large piece of it hit him in the chest, killing him instantly. Other bits wounded the earl of Angus and several gunners.

As the art of casting and metallurgy improved,

hooped guns went out of fashion, until by the end of the fifteenth century beautiful long guns of bronze had completely superseded them. But whether they were cast or welded, from about 1370 to 1380, guns became bigger and capable of throwing much heavier balls. The little early cannon had fired small balls that were not expensive to cast in metal, but with the great guns of the 1380s, it was a different matter. Copper or lead balls would be far too expensive, and even iron ones would not be cheap enough. So they were made of stone. If you look over an old European castle, you may see such stone balls often in piles. In Shakespeare's "Henry V," we are reminded of the use of stone in this fashion when the king replies to the French ambassadors who brought the dauphin's sarcastic gift of tennis balls: "And tell the pleasant Prince, this mock of his/Hath turned his balls to gunstones..."

These balls often weighed as much as 200 and 300 pounds apiece. Stone balls begin to appear in the English Wardrobe Accounts between 1382 and 1388, when the Keeper of the Wardrobe is found buying four great copper guns "made and ordered for shooting round stones" from a founder named William Woodward. At the same time he engaged a workman to work at the rounding of stones for cannon, and paid him a wage of 6 pence a day – the same as for a mounted archer. By 1399 the wages of a cannon-ball cutter had risen to around 1 shilling a day – the pay of a man-at-arms – so he must have been considered one of the most important of skilled workmen.

Despite the improved efficiency and larger size of cannon, it was not until about the middle of the fifteenth century that artillery really came into its own. There are a few isolated instances of towns being reduced by gunfire – Henry V's capture of Harfleur in 1414 is a good example – but it is not until later that the offensive power of cannon really began to overcome the age-long superiority of the strong castle or walled town.

In France European artillery received its biggest successes. Charles VII employed two gifted brothers, Jean and Gaspard Bureau, to equip forces with cannon in striving to throw the English out of France. The French seem to have been able to make better guns than anyone before them, for they began to take English castles and towns with great ease. At the siege of Harcourt in 1449 "the first shot thrown pierced completely through the rampart of the outer ward, which is a fine work and equal in strength to the keep." When the French reconquered Normandy in 1449-50, they besieged and took sixty places in a year and four days. Many places did not wait to be battered to pieces; as soon as they saw the big guns in position they gave up, for they knew it was hopeless to resist.

Guns were sometimes used on the field of battle during the earlier part of the fifteenth century. But they were only rarely effective, often because they were difficult to move once they were in position. After these guns were carefully placed and dug in, if a foe refused to fight on the prepared ground, the guns were useless.

It was, of course, the introduction of portable, small guns that had the greatest influence on the course of battles – and on the effectiveness of the knight. Late in the fourteenth century the "ribald" idea was seen as far more effective if each little tube were put in the hands of individual men, not all fastened together on a cart. So these little guns were mounted on spear-shafts. They were still slow, inaccurate, and ineffective, but the first step had been taken on the long road that has led to the modern rifle. These first hand-guns were fired by tucking the shaft under your arm, resting its tail on the ground behind you and firing off the piece with a match – the "match" being a length of cord impregnated with saltpeter and sulphur so that it smoldered slowly and continuously.

These guns could only be fired at a high trajectory and it was nearly impossible to aim them, so soon a far better device was brought in. The tube was clamped to a short shaft, more like a gunstock (fig. 56). This could be rested against the chest or shoulder, and the gun could be aimed. Not that it was accurate, even at close range; but a lot of these weapons fired off together in volleys could be highly effective. They were certainly unpopular, both with the old-style feudal knights and

Fig. 56. Hand-gun man. From a sculpture in Linköping Cathedral in Sweden, c. 1470

the canny professional soldiers of the "Free Companies" and "Condottas." In Italy these professional condottieri evolved a scheme of warfare that practically eliminated bloodshed for a time. There were fights, yes – splendid, clashing, colorful affairs like vast tournaments – but the contestants were covered in plate armor that prevented them from getting badly hurt, and the men they were fighting against – other professionals like themselves – might well become their comrades-in-arms the day after the fight. No point in antagonizing them. To the captain of a Condotta, a man such as Francesco Sforza or Carmagnola or Bartolomeo Colleoni, his men were his working capital; he would not risk getting it damaged or destroyed, so often battles were never fought. Much maneuvering would take place, then both sides would meet and look at the position they

103

were in; one would decide that he was outmaneu-
vered and beaten, and would march away.

But when hand-guns began to be used, things
were different. In 1439 the army in the pay of
Bologna used hand-guns against a force in the pay
of Venice, actually killing many of the Venetians'
knights. The Venetian army was so infuriated, it
won the battle and rounded up the Bolognese
army. Then the Venetians massacred the hand-gun
men who had stooped so low as to use this "cruel
and cowardly innovation, gunpowder." Why, they
said, if this sort of thing were allowed to happen,
war would become a positively dangerous busi-
ness.

Of course, war did become dangerous, for
nothing could arrest the march of progress that
made guns more effective and thus more lethal. As
hand-guns got better, more skilled men were
trained to use them. By the beginning of the sixteenth century, these guns were a potent force in
war, and the days of chivalry were over.

To the professional soldier, guns must have
been a godsend, but to the outmoded knight they
seemed utterly diabolical and disastrous. His traditional fierce courage, his dashing, glamorous dom-
ination of the battlefield, had suffered severe set-
backs from the halberds of Swiss and Flemish peasants and even more from the dreadful arrows of
English yeomen. But even these weapons had lost

some of their power over him, and he seemed to be on the verge of new and even more splendid successes since the armorers had devised for him the most effective, as well as the most beautiful, armor. Clad in smooth, gleaming iron (not steel—armor was made of very high quality iron) from head to foot, each piece in itself beautifully shaped, a work of fine craftsmanship, he must have felt like one of the very gods of war. Certainly he looked like one. Master of any infantryman who might come against him, almost entirely safe even from the cloth-yard shaft, beautiful as Apollo and terrible as Mars; yet it only needed a nasty little iron ball, fired from a crude tube by some insignificant little soldier using no skill, to tumble him from his horse into the dust, only the blood dulling the gleam of his armor around the ragged hole punched in it by the lowly ball to show how he met so inglorious an end.

Aptly did Shakespeare call this firepower "villainous saltpetre." Villainous it was and is. But the knightly code of courage and endurance had been proof against it, even if armor was not. A thing that astonished many people in those grim, brave days of the Middle Ages was the knights' extraordinary fearlessness and refusal to be beaten. When the men of the fourth Crusade in 1204 were assaulting Constantinople, the Byzantines were fearfully impressed by the ferocious courage of the

"Frankish" knights; nothing could stop these knights, the Greek chroniclers wrote, because they feared nothing. With utter disregard for life and limb they went on, taking no heed of wounds and not counting the number of their foes. They pressed on regardless of cost, and, because their only concern was victory, they generally won even against the most appalling odds. And if they died, that was how they wanted it. To meet the end in the heat and excitement of hand-to-hand conflict was what any dedicated knightly fighting man desired, and to make no fuss about being wounded was an essential part of his iron code.

Consider these words from the biography of a knight of Franconia, Götz von Berchlingen, who lost his hand in a fight outside Landshut in 1504. He says:

> On Sunday, while we were skirmishing under the walls of Landshut, the Nuremburgers turned their cannon upon friend and foe alike. The enemy had taken up a strong position on the dike, and I would fain have broken a spear with one of them. But as I held myself still and watched for the occasion, suddenly the Nuremburgers turned their cannon upon us; and one of them, with a culverin, shot in two my sword-hilt so that the one half entered into my right arm, and three armplates with it. The sword-hilt lay so deep in the armplates that it could not be seen. I marvel even now that I was not thrown from my horse. The

armplates were still whole; only the corners which had been bent by the blow stood forth a little. The other half of the sword-hilt and the blade were bent but not severed, and these, I believe, tore off my hand between the gauntlet and the vambrace; my arm was shattered behind and before. When I noticed that my hand hung loose by the skin, and that my spear lay under my horses' feet, I made as though nothing had happened to me, turned my horse quietly round, and in spite of all came safely back to my own people without hindrance from the enemy. Just then there came up an old spearman, who would have ridden into the thick of the fight. I called him to me, and asked him if he would stay by me, since he could see how things were with me. So he stayed, but soon he had to fetch the surgeon to me.

Götz lost his hand, but an armorer fitted him with an iron hand, not unlike one of our modern artificial ones; and "Götz of the Iron Hand" fought again in many a battle, siege, and foray until his death in 1562 at the age of eighty-two.

That's how it was with knights. And such bravery still may be. For even if the body is frailer than it once was, the human spirit is still as strong and fearless as ever, if given a chance.

*Fig. 57. Knight's sword, c. 1520.
Note the extra guards for the hand*

Glossary

Angon – the name Franks and Anglo-Saxons gave to the pilum, a throwing spear developed by the Romans and used to weigh down an enemy's shield.

Arquebus – a firearm that was portable.

Axe – one of the earliest weapons, made of different material and sizes. Popular among Vikings and their ancestors, but not favored among Celtic peoples.

Basilard – a two-edged dagger often carried with civil dress, though sometimes it was worn with armor.

Bayard, a.k.a. Pierre de Terrail – a French knight born in 1473. A highly skilled commander, he was known for exceptional fearlessness, heroism, and generosity. Was considered by many to be the ideal knight.

Besagew – an armor plate protecting an open area, as at the elbow or armpit.

Bill-hook – an agricultural tool for trimming hedges and chopping; it was mounted on a shaft and used as a weapon by infantrymen throughout the early part of the Middle Ages.

Bombard – a cannon.

Borgia, Cesare – member of a powerful Spanish family that planted roots in Italy. Born probably in Rome in either 1475 or 1476, he was the son of Rodrigo, a Roman Catholic cardinal who became Pope Alexander VI. Cesare Borgia gained political prominence and tried to use treachery to create a secular empire in central Italy. Machiavelli considered him a prime instance of the emerging new-style prince.

Buckler – a round shield, sometimes used by a knight to help him parry.

Carmagnola – born Francesco Bussone around 1390 and lived until 1432. An Italian condottiere born at Carmagnola, he worked in the service of the Duke of Milan and captured many cities. He commanded the Venetian force against Milan, was later convicted of treason, and beheaded.

Cast iron – commercial alloy of iron, carbon, and silicon. It's formed in a mold and is hard and not able to be hammered into shape (see wrought iron).

Champ clos – a small, square, fenced-off enclosure in which duels were fought to settle either affairs of honor or points of law.

Chappe – a flap that finished the lower part of the grip on some swords.

Chevalier – (French) a knight; person belonging to lowest rank of French nobility.

Colleoni, Bartolomeo – a famous fifteenth-century military entrepeneur in Italy who tried to establish a state in northern Italy in 1467 but was ultimately stopped.

Condottiere – a leader of mercenary armies in Italy, especially in the fourteenth and fifteenth centuries.

Cronel – special type of lance-head used in friendly jousts. It was crown-shaped.

Cultellus – name for a dagger from about 1000 to 1150.

Culverin – a medieval musket.

Dagger – a knife-like weapon but not always a short style of sword. There were many forms of medieval daggers, the earliest style from about 1000 to 1150 very much resembling the modern kitchen knife. Later daggers, though, were more shapely, and, by the second half of the fourteenth century, they developed long handles.

Dauphin – oldest son of a French king.

Dirk – a long dagger that developed from the kidney dagger.

English Civil War – a series of seventeenth-century battles in the British Isles between Parlimentarians and supporters of the monarchy.

Falchion – sword with curved blade used throughout the Middle Ages, mainly by infantrymen but occasionally by knights.

Francisca – the little throwing axe of the Franks.

Fuller – channel of a sword that runs down from the handle, often reaching close to the point.

Gisarme – large and beautiful spear that reached full development around 1470.

Glaive – weapon that resulted from the marriage of the billhook with spear; it had a long spike in front and a shorter one in back.

Godendag – literally "good morning," the name the Flemings gave to halberds that cut through mail and clove shields and helmets.

Graper – a part fastened around the lance behind the hand grip when queue was used with armor to help provide balance for lance.

Greave – armor for shin and calf.

Greek fire – a partly explosive and fiercely burning compound of now unknown composition used in medieval warfare.

Haft – word used for poles upon which axes, halberds,

glaives, and similar weapons were mounted. Not used for spears and lances.

Halberd – weapon that emerged along with the glaive, from the marriage of the bill-hook and spear. Halberd had a broad, short blade on a five-foot haft.

Hammer – a weapon that, along with the axe and mace, formed part of a knight's secondary armament. One style was known as a war hammer.

Harfleur – seaport in the north of France.

Hewing spear – a variety of spear used by the Vikings and their predecessors.

Hilt – handle of a sword.

Holy water sprinkler – type of mace with a ball and chain on a shaft.

Hooped gun – cannon with hoops around it that went out of fashion as casting and metallurgy improved. By the end of the fifteenth century, it had been superseded by long guns.

Hundred Years' War – series of wars from 1337 until 1453 pitting England against France, resulting ultimately in the English losing all colonial possessions in France except Calais.

Joust – a combat between two knights on horseback using lances.

Kidney dagger – a popular form of dagger usually with a back-edged blade and often worn with civil dress.

Lance – a spear and the quintessential knightly weapon, the long lance was used for jousting.

Latten – a type of brass set in the form of short bits of wire into slots in sword blades and, along with silver, tin, or copper, was used in inscribing letters on the weapon.

Legionary – member of a Roman army of foot soldiers.

List – an arena for jousting or, less specifically, the field of a competition, a controversy, or combat.

Longbow – archery weapon with great distance that, along with the yard-long arrow, helped lead to complete, close-fitting armor.

Lug – wing on the side of a partisan, springing from the blade itself. In a different form, it is a wing on the side of the winged spear, in which the lugs are separate from the blade and placed below it on the socket.

Mace – weapon that started off in remote times as a club. It developed into an armor-breaking weapon and took on various shapes, many beautiful in form. Flanges on mace were eventually capable not just of denting armor, but of piercing it.

Mantlet – shield for a gunner.

Morning star – type of mace, an infantry weapon with spikes sticking from it.

Partisan – popular name for a gisarme, this spear had a big head, like a great, broad sword blade and was generally 30 inches long.

Pence – plural of penny.

Pennon – distinctive flag on the lance of a knight.

Pike – a long infantry spear used for thrusting. The shaft was often as long as eighteen feet.

Pilum – a throwing spear developed by the Romans. It had a small, leaf-shaped head set on a long iron neck. It was used often to weigh down an enemy's shield.

Poll-axe – a weapon that came into use in the fourteenth century, the poll-axe was used by knights for fighting on foot. It was what its name implies, an axe for smashing heads or "polls," though wonderful workmanship was often evident in the design of the weapon. It didn't gain extreme popularity among knights until the middle of the fifteenth century.

Pommel – large knob on top of handle providing balance for sword by essentially acting as a weight to counterbalance the weight of the blade.

Queue – a tail fitted to the backplate of armor projected about a foot or more out of the right side of the back.

Quintain – contraption made by setting a vertical post in the ground. It was used for training to fight with a lance.

Ranseur – name for any kind of bill-like weapon.

Rapier – a thrusting sword.

Ribald – a nest of little guns, a series of tubes or barrels clamped together with the touch-holes arranged so that a single match would set them all off.

Robert the Bruce – he lived from 1274 until 1329 and is a hero to Scottish patriots. When Scottish independence had seemed imminent in 1306, he fled to Scotland. He murdered a rival to the Scottish throne and was crowned King Robert I at Scone on March 27, 1306.

Roundel – piece on a poll-axe protecting the leading hand of its user.

Runka – a type of spear.

Sabaton – metal footwear.

Saint George – an early Christian martyr and the patron saint of England. Little with certainty is known of him, but his heroic deeds date from the sixth century. He lived probably in the third century, but he was not known in England until the eighth. The legend of his saving a maiden from a dragon surfaced in the twelfth century and is a common theme in art.

Saracen – a nomad, often one on the Syrian borders of the Roman Empire; sometimes refers to a Muslim during the time of the Crusades (in the eleventh, twelfth, and thirteenth centuries).

Sax – sword favored by the Vikings and a precursor to the falchion.

Scabbard – a sheath in which a weapon, usually a dagger or sword, is contained. Often attached to a person and used for carrying the dagger or sword about.

Sforza, Francesco – a great condottiere of fifteenth-century Italy who overthrew, by 1450, the republican government of Milan and thus helped usher in a new despotism.

Shaft – word used for the poles upon which lances and spears were mounted.

Shilling – English monetary unit. It's equivalent to 12 pence or one-twentieth of a pound sterling.

Surcoat – an outer cloak, usually worn over armor.

Sporran – a pouch or purse.

Standard – banner serving as a rallying point or emblem, often containing the signature mark for a member of royalty, a head of state, a country.

String spear – spear thrown by a loop of cord wound round the shaft.

Sweyn Forkbeard – Sweyn I, called Forkbeard, was king of Denmark and eventually of England. He increased Viking attacks on England in 994, demanding enormous sums. By 1013 he conquered England and was made king. He died a year later.

Tang – a narrow tongue finishing a sword, helping the hilt or handle stay fastened to the blade.

Themistocles – an Athenian general and public official who lived from approximately 524 B.C. until 459 B.C. He supported expansion of the navy and trumpeted the lower classes. He often is given credit for protecting Greece from the Persians.

Thirty Years' War – central European war lasting from 1618 until 1648. At the start, it was between German Protestants and Catholics, but it ended up involving France, Sweden and Denmark against the Holy Roman Empire and Spain.

Vambrace – piece of protecting metal from the elbow to the wrist.

Vamplate – guard on the handle of certain lances.

Vouge – name for a spear, probably the same weapon as the glaive.

Wrought iron – a commerical form of iron that is somewhat soft and can be hammered into shape (see cast iron).

Bibliography

Blair, Claude. *European Armour.* Batsford, 1958.

Boccia, Lionello G. and Coelho, Eduardo T. *Armi Blanche Italiano.* Milano, 1975

Cripps Day, F. H. *Fragmenta Armamentaria.* 6 vols. Privately printed. Frome and London, 1934-56.

Crossley, A. H. *English Church Monuments* 1150-1550. 1921.

Dehio, G., and Bezold, G. V. *Die Denkmäler der deutschen Bildauerkunst.* 3 vols. Berlin, 1905.

Edge, David and Paddock, John Mills. *Medieval Knight.* London, 1986.

ffoulkes, C. J. *The Armourer and His Craft from the 11th to the 15th Century.* London, 1912.

Fryer, A. C. *Wooden Monumental Effigies.* 1924.

Gardner, A. *Alabaster Tombs.* Cambridge, 1940. *Medieval Sculpture in France* 1931.

Gay, Victor. *Glossaire Archéologique.* Paris, 1887.

Goldschmidt, A. *Die Skulpturen von Freiburg und Wechselburg.* 1924.

Harmand, Adrien. *Jeanne d' Arc: Ses Couturnes, Son Armure. Essai de Reconstruction.* Paris, 1929.

Hewitt, John. *Ancient Armour and Weapons in Europe.* 3 vols. London and Oxford, 1855-60.

Kelly, F. M., and Schwabe, Rudolph. *A Short History of Costume and Armour.* 1066-1800. 2 vols. London, 1931.

Koch, H. W. *Medieval Warfare.* London, 1985.

Laking, Sir G. F. *A Record of European Armour and Arms through Seven Ages.* 5 vols. London, 1920-22.

Mann, Sir James. Wallace Collection Catalogue, European Arms and Armour. 2 vols. London, 1962.

Muller, H., Kolling, H., and Platow, G. *Europaische Hieb-Und-Stichwappen.* Berlin, 1981.

Oakeshott, Ewart. *Records of the Medieval Sword.* Woodbridge, 1991.

- - -. *The Sword in the Age of Chivalry.* Second Edition. London & Woodbridge, 1995.

- - -. *The Archaeology of Weapons.* Second Edition. London & Woodbridge, 1995.

- - -. *European Weapon, Armour.* London, 1984.

Prior, E. S., and Gardner, A. *An Account of Medieval Figure Sculpture in England.* Cambridge, 1921.

Reverseau, Jean-Pierre. *Les Armes et la vie.* Paris, 1982.

Schneider, Hugo. *Waffen in Schweizerichen Landesnoseum Griffwaffen I.* Zurich, 1980.

Thomas, Bruno. *Deutsche Plattnerkunst.* Munich, 1944.

Thomas, B., and Gamber, O. *Die Innsbrucker Plattnerkunst.* Innsbruck, 1954.

Trapp, Osward Graf, and Mann (Sir) J. G. *The Armoury of the Castle of Churburg.* London, 1929.

Thordemann, Bengt. *Armour from the Battle of Visby* (in English). Stockholm, 1939.

Valencia, Conde de. Catalogo Historico-descriptivo de la Real Armeria de Madrid. Madrid, 1898.

PERIODICALS

The following are the most important periodicals dealing with arms and armour:

American Arms Collector. Towsen, Md., 1957 (in progress).

Armi Antichi. Bolletino del ' Accademia di S. Marciano. Turin, 1954 (in progress).

Journal of the Arms and Armour Society. London, 1953 (in progress).

Livrustkammaren. Journal of the Royal Armoury of Stockholm. 1937 (in progress).

Svenska Vapenhistoriske Aarskrift. Journal of the Swedish Arms and
Armour Society. Stockholm (in progress).

Vaabenhistoriske Aarbøger. Journal of the Danish Arms and Armour
Society. Copenhagen (in progress).

Zeitschrift für Historische Waffen- und Kostümkunde. Quarterly organ
of the now defunct Verein für Historische Waffenkunde. 17
vols. Dresden and Berlin, 1897-1944. Now revived as the
quarterly organ of the Gesellschaft für Historische Waffen- und
Kostümkunde. 1959 (in progress).

INDEX

A

Accolade, 90
Aboubement, 89
Age of Chivalry, 63, 73
Agincourt, 16
Alexander the Great, 23
Anglo-Saxons, 21, 41
Angon, 21, 43
Archer, 7,10-16, 98, 100
Armor, mail, 32, 66-67, 78
  plate, 33, 36, 68-69, 78, 103
Arquebus, 24-25
Austria, 30-32
Axe, 21, 26, 41-48, 63, 72, 88, 92,
  figs. 14-21

B

Bannockburn, 22
Bayard, 90
Belt-fittings, sword, 86 , fig. 46
Berchlingen, Götz von, 106
Besagew, 52
Bicocca, battle of, 24
Bill-hook, 25-26, 34, 43, 47, fig. 7,
  see also Glaive
Black Prince, the, 16, 18, 33, fig. 1
Boar-hunting, 39
Bologna, 103
Bolts, 96
Borgia, Cesare, 40
Bronze Age, 54, 85
Buckler, 69, 72
Bureau, Jean and Gaspard, 101
Bury St. Edmunds, 47
Byzantines, 105

C

Cannon, 25, 95-101, 106
  balls, 95, 97-98, 100
Canterbury, 17-18
Carmagnola, 103
"Cart of War", 97
Celts, 19, 42
Champ clos, 49
Chandos, John, 10, 12, 14
Chappe, 82-83, 85, fig. 44
Charlemagne, 43, 81, fig. 41
Chester, Earl of, 45-46
Colleoni, Bartolomeo, 103
Condottas, 103
Constantinople, 105
Courtrai, battle of, 29
Crécy, 16, 33
Cronel, 35
Crossbowmen, 17, 97
Crusade, the Fourth, 105

D

Dagger, 57, 62, 72, 90-94, figs. 47-53
  Basilard, 92 , fig. 49
  dirk, 94
  kidney, 92-93 , fig. 50
  Quillon,94, fig. 53
  Rondel, 93, fig. 52
  Scottish, 93, fig. 51
de Caimes, William, 47
de Grailly, Sir Jean, 12
de Hoveden, Roger, 46
de Terrail, Pierre, 90
duc d'Orléans, 9

121

E

English Civil War, 17, 74
Egyptians, 54

F

Falchion, 80-81, figs. 40-42
Fencing, 63, 72
Firearms, 95-96
Flemings, 29-30
Francisca, 43, fig. 15
Franks, 21-22, 41, 43
Free Companies, 103
Froissart, Jean, 87
Fuller, 77-79, fig. 37A

G

Gisarme, 27
Glaive or bill, 26-27, fig. 8
Gloucester, Earl of, 25, 45-46
Godendags, 30
Graper, 35
Greek fire, 95
Guns, 95-104
    hand, 102, 104, fig. 56
    hooped, 99-100, fig. 55
Gunpowder, 96, 104
Gunstones, 95, 99

H

Halberd,26-33, 51, 104 ,fig.9
Hammer, 17, 41-42, 48, 63
    poll-hammer, 50-53, 63, fig. 25
    war hammer, 52, fig. 24
Harfleur, 101
Harcourt, siege of, 101
Henry V, 34, 65, 100-101
Holy Roman Empire, 30

Holy Water Sprinkler, 56
Hundred Years' War, 16, 37, 92, 96

I

Inscriptions in sword-blades, 73-79

J

James II of Scotland, 99
Javelin, 21
Jean the Good Fellow, 14
Joust, 17, 33, 35-37
    à plaisance, 35

K

King Francis I of France, 90
King Jean of France, 10
King Stephen of England, 45
Knighthood, 29, 88-90

L

Lance, 11, 13, 17, 19-21, 26,29, 33-41, 50, 52, 72, fig. 11
    of courtesy, 35
Leopold, Duke of Austria, 30
Lincoln, battle of, 45-46
Locket, 85-87
Longbow, 32-33
    yard-long arrows, 32

M

Mace, 17, 23, 41, 51, 53-56, 62, 72, 88, 92, figs. 26-29
Macedonians, 23
Mail, *see* Armor
Marignano, battle of, 90

Maupertuis village, 14
Middle Ages, 22-26, 34, 36, 54,
    72, 80, 84-85, 105
Morgarten, battle of, 29-30
Morning Star, 56

N

New Stone Age, 19, 42
Nouaillé woods, 7

P

Partisan, 28, fig. 10
Pharaoh, 19, 23
Pike, 23-26, 33, figs. 5-6
Pilum, 20-21, 24, fig.3
Plantagenet, Edward, 7
Plate armor, see Armor
Plates, coat of, 29, 32-37
Poitiers, 13-17, 22, 37
poll-axe, 48-53, 63, 73 , figs. 22-23
Pommel, sword, 17, 53, 57-58, 70-
    73, 79-85
    dagger, 91, 94
Pot de Fer, 96, 97, fig. 54
Prince of Wales, 7, 16
Pydna, battle of, 24

Q

Queen Matilda, 45
Queue on backplate, 35
Quintain, 38

R

Ranseur, 27
Rapier, 72
Rest, lance, 35
Ribalds, 97

Ring, running at the, 39
Ring, sword carried in, 63
Roundel, 50
Roxburgh Castle, 99
Runka, 27

S

Sabaton, 38
Salisbury, Earl of, 10-11
Samurai warrior, 67-68
Sax, Viking, 80, fig. 39
Saxons, 22
Scabbard, 17, 63, 83-87
Scots, 22
Sforza, Francesco, 103
Shield, 20-22, 30, 35-37, 66, 69,
    97
Spear, 19-28, 35, 39-42, 50,
    figs. 2-4
    boar, 39, fig. 13
    hewing, 21
    string, 21
    Viking, 21
Sporran, 93
Standard, 46
Swiss, 24, 29-32, 104
Sword, 7, 17, 40, 43, 57-89,
    figs. 30-46, 57
    arming, 62
    assembling, 83-85, fig. 45
    basic design, 78-79, fig. 30
    belt-fittings, 86
    Black Prince's, the, 18
    blade sections, 78-79,
        figs. 37,38
    carried in ring, 63
    chained, 87
    fighting with, 63-67, 71, fig. 33

grip, 61, 81, 84-85, fig. 43
hilt, 34, 52, 85, fig. 43
"Hand-and-a-half", 61
inscriptions, 73-79, figs. 34,35
Japanese, 67-68
knot, 87
parrying with, 70-71
short, 24, 62
smiths' marks on, 78, fig. 34
tang, 84
thrusting, 68, 72
two-handed, 60-61
war, 60, fig. 31D

T

Tower of London Armories, 28

Thirty Years' War, 22

V

Vamplate, 34-35, 50-52
Vikings, 21-22, 41-45, 74-75, 80, 89, fig. 34
age of, 74
Vouge, 27

W

Warwick, Earl of, 10-13
Welsh, 22

Y

Yeoman warders, 28

Also in the Medieval Knight series
available from Dufour Editions

A Knight and His Castle

Second Edition
EWART OAKESHOTT

From the author's famous life of a medieval
knight series, this book provides a lively and
informative history of the castle, its design,
building, defense, as well as its armory,
daily life, and the training of knights.

*1996, glossary, illustrations,
index, 5½ x 8½, 128 pages,
Paper ISBN 0-8023-1294-2*

TO ORDER CALL DUFOUR EDITIONS AT 1-800-869-5677